Contents

Part D: Managing people

Part E: Managing the employment relationship

ACTION
MANAGEMENT:
THE ESSENTIALS

£12·95

ACTION MANAGEMENT: THE ESSENTIALS

by

Derek Torrington and Jane Weightman

Institute of Personnel Management

3 0 3

First published in 1991

© Derek Torrington and Jane Weightman 1991

Photoset by James Jenkins Typesetting
577 Kingston Road, Raynes Park, London SW20
and printed in Great Britain
by Short Run Press, Exeter

British Library Cataloguing in Publication Data
Torrington, Derek, 1931-
Action management.
I. Title II. Weightman, Jane
658

ISBN 0 85292 473 9

Introduction

This is a rather specialized book for practising managers of all types. We believe you, the reader, are a manager who does not yet know all the answers. We believe also that you do not like reading management books. You are busy, with little time and patience for extended, thoughtful discussion on the issue of management. To you management is action, getting things done and tackling problems as they present themselves, while reading books is passive and reflective. You will read reports and memoranda, and will read the odd article in a management journal, but reading books and doing the job of management will seem to you activities that sit uneasily together.

If we have so far given a fairly accurate description of yourself, we suggest you read the rest of this introductory chapter to see if this book can be of use to you.

In working out our ideas we gave this book two complementary nicknames: 'briefcase book' and 'cookery book'. We regard it as a briefcase book because we hope you will put it in your briefcase to read bit by bit while on trains or waiting at airports, or to look up something when going through figures or before attending a meeting. We do not expect you to sit down and read it from start to finish. It is designed to be read piecemeal, without the risk of losing the thread of any argument.

The term 'cookery book' is usually a term of abuse among management academics for texts that tell people how to do things, but we hope we have avoided the pitfall of being trite by providing solid and compact explanations of *why* methods should work as well as *how* to make them work. The main content is recipes for dealing with practical events, from the relatively straightforward task of report writing to the mysteries of dealing with organizational politics, the subtleties of counselling and the statistical precision of sampling methods.

Each chapter is a self-contained unit and all are presented in the following common format of four pages:

Page 1:   Background information and explanation of the area of management action being described.

Pages 2 & 3: Brief explanatory material such as check-lists, condensed information, guidance notes and various recipes.

Page 4:   Practical exercises, suggestions for further reading, and a final word on the topic.

The chapter topics are arranged in five parts:
A.   Managing oneself
B.   Managing in the organization
C.   Managing to get things done
D.   Managing people
E.   Managing the employment relationship

This book is a successor to an earlier IPM publication, *Management Methods*, published in 1985 and written in conjunction with our erstwhile colleague, Kirsty Johns. Some of her original thinking has been retained in this volume.

We have sought to combine an academic study of management processes with our own personal experiences of managerial work and the working environment. The main basis of what we are writing is our extensive reading of management literature and detailed research among managers in a large number of very different organizations. This is reinforced and put into perspective by extensive working experience in areas as diverse as engineering and education.

We believe the methods we describe will work in most real-life situations. They may not be precisely correct for your particular situation, but they should be sufficient as guidelines to provide a practical, and not simply a theoretical, basis for action.

Part A

Managing oneself

1 Personal credibility

People with high credibility are convincing, trustworthy and respected. They are listened to and can get things done willingly by other people, while their colleagues who lack credibility meet resistance and have to rely on formal mechanisms to get things done. For managers to remain effective they have to earn and maintain credibility with those working in the same department or unit. It is only by keeping in touch with the main task and retaining a down to earth quality that they can ensure that new ideas are based on reality and that there is a ready-made network to put changes into practice.

It is useful to distinguish between two types of possession of authority: being *in* authority and being *an* authority (Carter, 1979). The first, which is having a position of authority, requires support whereas the latter stands on its own. Being an authority is having the skill, knowledge and expertise that others consult willingly. We found in our research on middle managers (Torrington and Weightman, 1987) that credibility within units was dependent on being *an* authority about the main task of that unit, whether it was engineering, telecommunications, selling, purchasing, flying airplanes or educating children. Managers who lose touch with the expertise which is the basis of the operation they manage are in danger of losing credibility in the eyes of their colleagues. They then have difficulty in getting things done. Credibility is not a right that comes with the job nor is it an intrinsic quality of the individual. It has first to be earned and then constantly maintained by each person in each job – all the time.

Power and authority in organizations also depend on legitimacy. We only have as much power and authority as is allowed to us by those among whom we seek to exert that power. Various devices are used within organizations to legitimize power and authority. The formal organization charts, job titles and pay structures are one such device, the demonstration of leadership is another, but the organizations of Western society have developed a taste for informal means of legitimizing authority. Managers therefore have to establish the legitimacy of their position by the credibility they can earn informally by their expertise, by working hard, developing a good network of contacts, showing enthusiasm and being willing to do things.

Managers who have a good network of contacts and who are credible with colleagues are more likely to be able to consult about new projects effectively. They are also likely to know when things begin to go wrong rather than finding out too late. Managers who rely on formal relationships and who lack credibility will be told only what they expect to hear, and then only when they have to be told.

Sources of power

---

1. Position

- *Resources.* Control access to what others need; whether subordinates, peers or superiors, it includes the following: materials, information, rewards, finance, time, staff, promotion, references.

- *Delegation.* Whether jobs are pushed down the hierarchy; with rights of veto retained or not.

- *Gatekeeper.* Control information, relax or tighten rules, make life difficult or easy depending on loyalty of individuals.

2. Expertise

- *Skill.* Being an expert. Having a skill others need or desire.

- *Uncertainty.* Those who have expertise to deal with a crisis become powerful till it is over.

- *Indispensable.* Either through expertise or by being an essential part of the administrative process.

3. Personal qualities

- *Motivation.* Some seek power more enthusiastically than others.

- *Physical prowess.* Being bigger or stronger than others . . . Not overtly used in management except as controller of resources. However, statistically the leaders tend to be taller than the led.

- *Charisma.* Very rare indeed. Much discussed in early management literature as part of leadership qualities, but usually control of resources can account for claims of charismatic power.

- *Persuasion skills.* Bargaining and personal skills that enable one to make the most of one's other powers, such as resources.

4. Political factors

- *Debts.* Having others under obligation for past favours.

- *Control of agenda.* Coalition and other techniques for managing how the issues are, or are not, presented. Being present when important decisions are taken, control of minutes.

- *Dependence.* Where one side depends on the other for willing cooperation, the power of removal exists. Strikes or threatening to resign *en bloc* are two examples.

(Source: Torrington and Weightman, *1989*.)

How can credibility be enhanced?

How can your credibility in your present position be enhanced? Here are some possibilities:

- making your role and duties better known to people;
- taking care not to flaunt your privileges;
- reviewing your contribution to the organization to be sure that it matches your privileges;
- sharing privileges, while taking care not to be condescending. ('Can you help me with the timetable . . .?' is very different from 'Providing you don't make a mess, you can use my kettle when I don't need it.')

The example illustrated below may offer some further ideas.
  Now decide on two or three things to do in the next fortnight.

Signs of authority in organizations	
Being IN authority	**Being AN authority**
Job title	Being referred to as 'our Mr/Ms . . .'
Position in hierarchy	
Being the necessary signatory for expense claims and similar authorizations	Having one's advice genuinely sought for its value, not just as a formality
Being a person to whom people other than direct subordinates report	Being able to work with considerable latitude for independent decision-making
Chairing meetings or committees	Having confidence in what one is doing; not needing constant reassurance or guidance

Your Management Action

Exercises

1. What is the basis of your credibility at work? How much of this is based on things you did before this year?
2. What is your expertise? How do you ensure that this is still relevant?
3. Is there any evidence in recent weeks of your lacking credibility? Forget your paranoia or self doubts and think of tangible evidence. Write it down. What aspects of your role is it related to?
4. What sources of power do the following have? They may have more than one.
    The Queen; the Prime Minister; Mick Jagger; the leader of the TUC; a newsreader; your boss; yourself.

Further reading

Carter, A. *Authority and Democracy*, Routledge and Kegan Paul, London, 1979.

Torrington, D.P. and Weightman, J.B. 'Middle Management Work', *Journal of General Management*, Vol.13, No.1, pp.20-32, Blackwell, Oxford, 1987.

Torrington, D.P. and Weightman, J.B. *The Reality of School Management*, Blackwell, Oxford, 1989.

And finally . . .

An example of gaining credibility

William Barnes was a well-established school with very low staff turnover. Most of the staff had spent all their teaching career (often more than 20 years) in the school. The Deputy Head/Pastoral was a pillar of this establishment who dealt loudly and clearly with discipline problems amongst the children. Staff relied on him to back them up and felt secure that discipline would be firm. He retired at the end of the summer term and Derek arrived as his replacement the following September.

Derek was 33, younger than most of the staff, and he was appointed from outside the school and its immediate neighbours. He was tall, dark and handsome. By the time the researchers arrived in November, Derek had established a lot of respect. Teachers kept saying, 'You must go and see Derek, he's marvellous.' In terms of credibility with the staff, Derek had 'a tough act to follow'. How had he done it?

The basis of his acceptance was lots of small, but important things:

*   *He was reliable – if he said he would do something he did it.*
*   *He was consistent, treating people and issues fairly and predictably.*
*   *He established order where it had previously been lacking, such as instigating systems for reports and examination entries.*
*   *He was visible, regularly walking about in the building, playground, dining room.*
*   *He took up individual problems but only after checking that the appropriate system, procedure or person had been tried first.*

2   Management work

The work of managers has been defined traditionally as the art of getting things done through people, but this is not limited to managers. All those who organize human affairs have management work to do. Teachers, orchestral conductors, parents, ambassadors, chefs, bishops, senior systems analysts and many others all have a management ingredient to their jobs, but they are unlikely to emphasize it and may not even recognize it. Managing may not be central to their work, but it enables the job to get done.

The work of managers has been studied carefully in the last 40 years and it will be no surprise to managers reading this book that most studies show the manager's day to be characterized by constant interruptions, brief periods of specialized activity and constant switching from one task to another. Management work is not a serene activity of continuous, thoughtful planning and assimilation of reports. There is continual change, and most managers spend between 50 and 80 per cent of their time talking to other people.

Kotter (1982) gives a useful definition of the core behaviours of managers as that of first setting agendas for action and then establishing and maintaining networks to implement those agendas. Agendas are lists of things to be done. These agendas are implemented through a network of contacts. This is dealt with further in chapters 16 and 17 and a more detailed analysis of management work is shown below. The effective manager is the one who has both a useful agenda and an appropriate network. We can all think of individuals who know just what to do (agenda) but are hopeless with people (network); or others who are good with people but do not know what needs doing.

The nature of management work varies with the job. Differentiation by function groups together those activities that are associated with production, marketing, personnel or some other functional division of the management process, so that the grouping and identification of the managers is according to their specialist expertise. Management work also varies with level in the hierarchy. Top managers are those at the apex of the organizational pyramid, like a board of directors, who have few but vital responsibilities concerning the overall direction of the business, like merger, acquisition and closure. Senior managers are concerned with policy formulation and implementation. The initial stages of implementation are likely to produce major problems and queries, and this is the main reason why the lives of senior managers tend to be frenetic. Middle managers complete the process of implementation within the organization and try to resolve the unintended consequences of the policies themselves. Supervisory managers arrange for the work for which the organization exists to be done: making cars, running the sales office, producing ice cream, making up hotel beds and so forth, in other words dealing with the day-to-day variations and demands.

The 10 roles of the manager

Formal authority
and status

INTERPERSONAL ROLES

1. *Figurehead,* to represent the unit formally.
2. *Liaison,* to deal with peers and outsiders in order to swap information.
3. *Leader,* to staff the unit and motivate its members.

INFORMATIONAL ROLES

4. *Monitor,* to gather and store information useful to the unit.
5. *Disseminator,* to pass on to subordinates information not otherwise available.
6. *Spokesperson,* to pass out information from the unit.

DECISIONAL ROLES

7. *Entrepreneur,* to initiate change.
8. *Disturbance handler,* to take charge when the unit is threatened.
9. *Resource allocator,* to decide where and how unit resources will be deployed.
10. *Negotiator,* to deal with outsiders whose consent and cooperation is required by the unit.

The composition of the manager's incoming mail

	%
Reports on operations	18
Periodical news	15
Reference data	14
Status requests	12
General reports	8
Events	8
Advice on situations	6
Solicitations	5
Authority requests	5
Acknowledgements	5
Ideas	2
Problems and pressures	2

Distribution of hours and activities in the chief executive's work

Hours spent   *Number of activities*

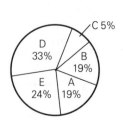

A   Scheduled meetings
B   Unscheduled meetings
C   Tours
D   Desk work
E   Telephone calls

(Source: Mintzberg, *1973.*)

An alternative method of classifying management jobs

- *Hub* jobs have necessary contact with subordinates, superiors and peers. It is the most common type of job and has a dominant human management component.

- *Peer dependent* jobs are those with less 'vertical' demand and much dependence on winning the cooperation of peers. Often found on the boundaries of organizations.

- *Man management* jobs are those concerned primarily with the vertical type of working relationship, having contact mainly with superiors and subordinates.

- *Solo* jobs are those of managers who spend a large part of their time working alone on assignments.

The gods of management

A more whimsical idea is that there are four gods of management that embody the philosophy, culture and structure of organizations or parts of organizations. Each person will have a preferred god, but each of the four can be useful in particular circumstances.

- *Zeus* The god of the club culture with a central figure, as in a spider's web. The mode of dynamic entrepreneurs who rule their empires on snap decisions.

- *Apollo* The god of the role culture, with everyone in their proper place doing prescribed jobs. The bureaucratic order often found in large organizations.

- *Athena* The goddess of the task culture, where expertise is the basis of power and influence. The matrix structure.

- *Dionysus* The god of the existential culture where role is based on personal relations without a defined boss. Found as a form of organizations among artists and some professionals.

(Sources: Stewart, *1967, 1976*; Handy, *1978.*)

Your Management Action

Exercises

1. Which god do you serve? Which one does your boss believe in? What are the consequences of differences in these views? How would you convert the boss to your view?
2. What is your agenda at the moment? Who is going to help you to achieve these things?
3. Michael Edwardes argues (1984) 'It is better to have a focal point of leadership which is crisp and sharp, than to wallow in consensus, which we do in Britain.' Which god does this fit in with?

Further reading

Edwardes, M. 'UK Squanders its Management Talent', *Chief Executive*, November 1984, 10–15.

Handy, C. *The Gods of Management*, Pan, London, 1978.

Kotter, J. *The General Managers*, The Free Press, New York, 1982.

Mant, A. *The Rise and Fall of the British Manager*, Macmillan, London, 1977.

Mintzberg, H. *The Nature of Managerial Work*, Harper and Row, New York, 1973.

Mintzberg, H. The Manager's Job: Folklore and Fact', *Harvard Business Review*, July/August 1975, 49.

Stewart, R. *Managers and Their Jobs*, Macmillan, London, 1967.

Stewart, R. *Contrasts in Management*, McGraw-Hill, Maidenhead, 1976.

And finally . . .

In understanding managerial work we must remember:

> *Management is a much less tidy, less organised, and less easily defined activity than that traditionally presented by management writers or in job descriptions.*

(Stewart, 1976, p.125.)

3   Analysing your own job

Analysing your own job can help you do it better by showing up the opportunities you are missing and the difficulties you are not overcoming. Our method is to distinguish between three types of work that managers do: *technical*, *administrative* and *managerial*, and consider the balance between the three. In addition managers have social and personal activities in a working day – which gives us the mnemonic 'sTAMp'.

- *Technical work* is what managers do because of their profession, experience or qualification. This kind of work is often done also by subordinates, and is the sort of work the manager did before being promoted to management. A manager is doing technical work when, for instance, a sales manager negotiates with a customer, when a senior nursing officer nurses a patient, or a hotel manager books in a client. Technical work is usually concerned with the main task of the unit or organization.

- *Administrative* work of managers is that concerned with organizational maintenance. It is work concerned with carrying out official, often regular duties, authorized by others, such as a boss or a committee. Managers are doing administrative work when, for instance, they calculate the hours worked by subordinates, check expenses or fill in weekly returns. Much of this is the sort of work 'any literate sixteen-year-old could do'.

- *Managerial* work is that of conducting organizational affairs with the freedom to create precedents. It is not usually the managerial work of deciding to make margarine or build bicycles but the smaller activities of nudging things along, persuading others to agree to a new line of action, or getting people to do things they would not otherwise have done.

Managers' jobs vary in the balance between these three types of work. This is partly because of the choices made by individual managers.

Managers abandon their technical work too easily in favour of administrative work. If they maintain their technical skills, they will keep in touch with the main task of the organization, have the satisfaction of using their technical skills, and are more likely to survive in times of company reorganization. Technical skills are readily transferable to different situations, but administrative skills are usually relevant only in the organizational context in which they have been acquired. Managers often retreat into administrative work because it is obvious and doing it gives the satisfaction of having completed something. It may be that the managerial work to be done is not clear, too difficult or taken over the boss. However, we all have some administration in our work; the question, as always, is one of balance.

How much managerial work does your job include?

Record how you spend your time at work for at least one day. A suggested format is set out below. Try to do it during the day in question and not later, so that you do not forget the small details. Every time you change an activity, start a new line. A change of activity is either moving to a new topic or a new person. Meetings count as one activity. Tick how the activity was initiated, how it was conducted and which of the broad category of skills was involved, as defined above.

		Initiative		Method			Type of work				
Time	Activity	Self	Other	Face to face	Phone	Alone	Soc	Tech	Admin	Managerial	Pers

The information collected can be used in various ways, including those suggested in the next chapter:

- Does your day fit that described in the last chapter as typical, with constant interruptions and only brief periods on any one topic?
- Are you surprised about the time distribution? How much of your day was spent responding to others?
- How much of your day was spent with other people?
- What proportion of your day was spent using technical skills, what proportion using administrative skills and what proportion using managerial skills?
- Is that distribution acceptable to you?

See if you can get greater control over your affairs by using the check-list below.

What choices do you have at work?

The choices you have at work are restricted by the demands and constraints of your job. However, every job involves some choices. You can analyse the choices available to you by looking at the following questions.

Demands

What are the demands of your job? That is the things that have to be done by you. They cannot be ignored, delegated or passed on. What are the penalties for not doing them? It might help to think of the following areas:

1. Subordinates
2. More senior members of staff
3. Peers
4. People outside the organization
5. Administration – procedures and meetings
6. Others

Constraints

What are the constraints that stop you developing your job in absolutely the way you would like? For example:

1. The resources, e.g. buildings
2. Legal or trade union
3. Technical limitations of equipment
4. Physical location
5. Organization policies and procedures
6. Attitude of others
7. Others

Choices

There are choices about *what* you do, *how* you do it and *when* you do it. What are the choices available to you?

1. Within your unit
2. With your peers
3. To protect the unit from disturbance
4. Upwards
5. Elsewhere in the organization
6. Outside the organization
7. Others

(Source: Stewart, 1982)

Exercises

1. Using the drills on the last two pages, compare your job with that of a colleague doing similar work. How different are your balances between technical, administrative and managerial work? What causes these differences? Are there ways in which you can exercise a greater degree of choice in your job?

2. Listed at the foot of the page are some advantages and disadvantages of technical, administrative and managerial work. Can you think of any more?

Further reading

Stewart, R. *Choices for the Manager*, McGraw-Hill, Maidenhead, 1982.

Torrington, D.P. and Weightman, J.B. 'Technical Atrophy in Middle Management', *Journal of General Management*, Blackwell, Oxford, vol. 8, no. 4, pp 5-17, 1982.

Torrington, D.P. and Weightman, J.B. 'Middle Management Work', *Journal of General Management*, Blackwell, Oxford, 1987.

And finally . . .

The balance of work for managers:

	Technical	**Administrative**	**Managerial**
Advantages	Authority of expertise	Easy to do	React quickly to differences between plan and reality
		Even pace	
	Keep in touch with subordinates' work	Keep things running smoothly	Make choices and decisions
	Pride in work		
	Task-oriented		
Disadvantages	Lose sight of overall aims of organization	Subordinates irked by demands	Hectic pace
			Erratic demands
	'Generalist' skills not developed	Comfort of doing something certain creates more administrative work	Lot of time spent building networks, which can become more important than getting the job done
	Subordinates may be denied scope if technical workload limited	Administrative work can become an end in itself	

4 Personal organization

Personal organization is about managing yourself effectively. By controlling your work consciously you become more aware of the choices to be made and consequently less passive. Personal organization is deciding what, how, where, when and with whom it needs doing. Why something is done is often dictated by others, the boss, committee, customer or colleagues, and is less a question of personal organization.

Busy managers often mention that their memory is worse than it once was. It is hardly surprising in a constantly interrupted, disjointed day that some facts and opinions are not recalled unless jotted down. Junior employees usually work for long periods on single tasks and so have more opportunity to store and rehearse the information relevant to the job. No training programme would ever organize information input to be constantly interrupted in the way a great deal of the manager's input is. Thus, the only way to remember much in these circumstances is to organize consciously.

Time is often seen to be in short supply by managers. There are several different aspects to this. Where a large number of different demands are made on a manager's time, priorities need to be set and some demands will have to be deferred or refused. Finding longer periods of time for collecting and organizing information, report writing and longer term projects is difficult to maintain when immediate demands are made which can be resolved immediately. However, some claims of pressure of time can be attributed to a lack of desire to do something.

Keeping paperwork under control is important. Many organizations have papers copied for large numbers of people partly to prevent the excuse of not being informed, and partly to maintain the political network. Consequently, most managers' in-tray will contain more papers than are strictly necessary for getting the job done. Add to this the comfort to be gained from doing something where the end is achievable, such as emptying the in-tray, and paperwork can take up a disproportionate amount of time and energy. The art is in keeping the paper organized.

One of the choices that managers cherish and protect is the right to control their own diaries. This can develop sometimes into a demonstration of relative status and power when trying to agree dates. Having decided when to meet, and with whom, the place for the meeting will be dictated by relative status and convenience. If you get the other person to come to you, less of your time is consumed, but the other person will have slightly more control over the time the meeting finishes.

The poorly organized manager responds to the initiatives of other people, and is dependent on them. A lack of preparation enables others to dominate, slows things down, produces errors and leads to dissatisfaction. Indications of this are the use of such phrases as 'I've just not had the time', 'Let's play this one by ear', 'I'm still waiting for . . .', 'I've tried to contact them but . . .', 'I'm sorry, I quite forgot about it'.

Memory

There are different types of memory. The main ones are:

1. *Recall*   which is being able to repeat the task, message, behaviour, without referring to notes. This type of memory is not always as accurate as we think.

2. *Recognition*   is being able to recognize or distinguish that the material is familiar. For example, when we look in the file and remember the problem we were having with the order from a supplier.

3. *Improved assimilation*   is the act of not recognizing something as familiar but understanding or learning much more quickly than the first time the material was encountered.

What level of memory is necessary? A lot of management work can be at the recognition level. For example, notes are consulted, the matter is dealt with and then forgotten.

- *Ways of improving recall*   Rehearse the material at the start. For example, repeat the name of the person you have just been introduced to. Practising helps memory.

- *Ways of improving recognition*   Keep an action list of what needs doing. Next to appointments in your diary put the topic to be discussed.

Time

Decide what the priorities are.
1. What *must* you do today, this week, this month, this year?
2. What *should* you do today, this week, this month, this year?
3. What do you *hope* to do today, this week, this month, this year?
4. What can be ignored, passed 'up', delegated 'down'?

Setting a pattern for the day can marshal time effectively, for example:
- Taking phone calls 9am – 11am
- Making telephone calls 2pm – 4pm
- Signing expense claims and letters 4:30pm – 5pm

This pattern can also work for the week.

Paperwork

1. *Filing*   Current material is usually in one folder, briefcase or tray. Most filing cabinets have a few bulging files and a larger number that are almost empty. A list of files can spread usage, because managers will then consult the list to find documents instead of relying on only those few files they can recall. Most file titles are by source, such as a file for each customer, or by use, such as a file for each committee.

    The 'just in case I should ever need it' can probably be thrown away, especially if it is likely to be retained in someone else's filing cabinet.

2. *Bring out systems*   are files by date, so that material is filed for review on a predetermined date, thereby avoiding pressure on the bulging current file and avoiding the risk of the matter being overlooked.

3. *Colour coding*   is a way of sorting paper, by using different colours for different purposes, with white for advice, pink for information and red for action. This usually fails because of the tendency for all memoranda soon to be typed on red paper!

There are a number of products on the market that provide a simple organizing element for the manager, e.g. organizer diaries and the Filofax system of small files with sheets to cover a variety of situations; and electronic systems.

Diaries

1. Mark preparation periods. For example, before an important meeting mark three days previously 'prepare for . . . meeting'.

2. Mark recurring items. For example, last Tuesday of every month 'returns in'.

3. Give talkative people an appointment just before lunch or a meeting so you both have an incentive to stop.

4. Remember travelling time.

5. If you are running very late why not phone and say so?

Your Management Action

Exercises

1. Have a look in the filing cabinet and count how many files you have used in the last week. How many have you not used in the last year?
2. When you are introduced to new people try saying their name, e.g. 'How nice to meet you Mrs . . .'.
3. Look at your action list – make one if you don't already have one – and mark it for 'must', 'should' and 'hope' for the next week.
4. Practise delegating both up and down, saving for yourself that work which only you can do.
5. If you were able to organize yourself better who would benefit?
6. List five ways in which you manage your boss. Could these be improved?

Further reading

Boursine, D.P. and Guerrier, Y. *Surviving as a Middle Manager*, Croom Helm, Beckenham, Kent, 1983.
Buzan, T. *Use Your Head*, BBC Publications, London, 2nd edn, 1982.
Pedler, M., Burgoyne, J. and Boydell, T. *A Manager's Guide to Self Development*, McGraw-Hill, Maidenhead, 2nd edn, 1986.

And finally . . .

Personal organization also means looking after your own interests. One way is to consider your goals for the future; personal, social, material and career. If these goals are different from where you are now, what can be done about it? One technique for career goals in management has been the development of programmes of self-development to increase skills and knowledge. See, for example, Pedler et al. (1986).

5 Interpersonal communication

Interpersonal communication is used here to describe the one-to-one or small group conversations in which managers spend most of their time. Effectiveness in these situations is one of the keys to successful management performance, as this is how managers get things done: a person is persuaded to follow a new invoice procedure, the logic of a new marketing plan is explained and justified, a problem is eased or enthusiasm engendered. There are briefing sessions and there are everyday conversations for social contact and stimulation that maintain smooth co-operative and personal relations. Each of these requires some variation of the manager's personal communications style and difficulties can arise if these varying demands are not understood.

Communication is a two-way process, complete only when the message is received and understood, even if the understanding is not exactly what was intended. Both the sender and receiver of a message have an active part to play. This reciprocal process is sometimes described as the speech chain and uses systems or information theory terms to describe the process. For effective communication to take place each of the following six stages needs to be operating well: encoding, transmitting, environment, receiving, decoding and feedback (see below). When we want to be effective communicators we need to consider not only our own performance but also that of those with whom we are communicating, and the likely effect upon them of what we are saying and how we are saying it. Understanding other people is difficult because we all have a set of operating assumptions to conduct our daily lives by, and we all have a different set. If we do not recognize this diversity, communication becomes at best awkward and at worst non-existent.

Factors other than those involved in the communication can also affect the outcome of a conversation or meeting. Physical things such as noise and temperature are obvious factors. The position of the furniture can also play a part. Seating a group so they can all see each other increases interaction. Having a table between participants increases the formality but gives them quite literally something to hold on to if it is a tense situation. Interruptions from the telephone or keeping an 'open door' disrupt communication.

Difficulties can occur because the purpose of the communication is unclear, because there are problems in the speech chain, or because of outside factors. Where effective communication is critical each stage needs to be considered in order to preempt any possible problems.

Methods of interpersonal communication

1. Getting started

Establish rapport, so that participants get used to each other's tone, volume and personality. Methods include: small talk, friendly manner, calm attention and explaining what is going to happen.

2. Keeping it going

Maintain rapport and keep the communication to the agenda. Methods include: showing interest, giving verbal and non-verbal signals of agreement, making encouraging noises but keeping silent at times when other people are considering points. It may sometimes be necessary to bring suppressed feelings into the open by asking a question like 'Is there something on your mind . . .?'

3. Questions

There are different types of question according to what you want to do:

Type	Purpose	Example
Closed	To seek precise information	'What is your name?'
Open	To get opinions developed	'How do you do that?'
Direct	To insist on a reply	'Why did you do that?'
Indirect	An oblique approach to a difficult matter	'What were they like?'
Probe	To obtain information that is being withheld. One way is to exaggerate	'You weren't in prison, were you?'
Proposing	To put forward an idea	'Shall we do as Tom suggests?'
Rhetorical	To forbid a reply	'We're not afraid of the competition, are we?'

4. Stopping

- Slow the general rate of talking by slipping one or two closed questions into the conversation and eliminating encouraging gestures.
- Gather your papers together and say something to indicate closing, such as 'Well, I think we have covered the ground . . .'
- Explain the next step, such as who does what.
- Stand up.

The basic communications model or speech chain

Stage	Process	Check points
ENCODING	Deciding on the message	Clarify your objectives
	Selecting the right words	What will the other person want from the message?
	Understanding the other person	What will be the emotional impact of the message?
TRANSMITTING	Selecting the right medium	Make sure there are no more than approximately 7 ideas to transmit
	Sending the message	
	Giving non-verbal signals	Are words and non-verbal signals consistent?
		Is the language suitable?
ENVIRONMENT	Coping with distractions	Avoid interruptions and noise
	Dealing with distortions	
		Is the seating right?
RECEIVING	Perceiving the message	What phrases, facts and inferences am I looking for?
	Listening actively	
		How can I test my understanding of the message?
DECODING	Making sense of the message	What do they mean?
		What is the 'hidden agenda'?
	Understanding the other person	How will I handle it if it does not fit in with my beliefs?
FEEDBACK	Encoding the response	To keep the communication going: nod, smile, agree
	Starting the next message	
		To stop the communication: look uninterested, stop eye contact

Your Management Action

Exercises

1. From a group of people ask two to leave the room to prepare a brief talk on their present occupations. Agree with the rest of the group to give positive feedback to the first and negative feedback to the second. Ask the two speakers to come in one at a time and give their talks. Discuss the reactions of the speakers and the audience's behaviour.

2. Which of the following seating arrangements do you think would be most appropriate for a counselling session, a union negotiation and a selection interview? Give your reasons.

Further reading

Argyle, M. *The Psychology of Interpersonal Behaviour*, Pelican, Harmondsworth, 1972.

Berne, E. *Games People Play*, Andre Deutsch, London, 1966.

Goffman, E. *The Presentation of Self in Everyday Life*, Penguin, Harmondsworth, 1972.

Torrington, D. P. *Face to Face in Management*, Prentice-Hall, London, 1991.

And finally...

Berne has made an interesting analysis of how we interact with each other. He proposes that each of us has within us behaviours that can be described as **parent,** **adult** *or* **child.** *When we communicate with others all combinations are possible. Two of the more common ones are:*

Complementary which is expected and appropriate Whenever the lines of communication are parallel understanding is easy

Crossed where the first statement gets an inappropriate response from the other person

6 Assertiveness

A few years ago a book was published called *If I'm in Charge, Why is Everybody Laughing?* This neatly summarizes the phobia of many managers that they will be pushed around, that they will not command respect. We began this book by discussing how managers can acquire credibility. In this chapter we describe how a person can become *assertive*, rather than being aggressive or diffident. Assertive people are those who avoid being pushed around and who obtain attention for their plans and projects as a result of their self-confidence. Aggression and diffidence are usually indications that the person demonstrating those behaviours lacks self-confidence.

> True assertiveness is a way of being in the world which confirms one's own individual worth and dignity while simultaneously confirming and maintaining the worth of others. (Bolton, *1987*, p.125.)

The value of assertiveness for managers is not simply that they avoid being pushed around; they also avoid pushing others around.

The need for assertiveness is partly a product of overcrowding. When people are crowded together, either literally in a rush hour bus or metaphorically in a busy organization, they get in each other's way, the individual finds it difficult to establish personal space and privacy, the weak are inhibited by the strong and all compete with each other for recognition, identity and achievement. When an organization is short of opportunities for its people to achieve their ambitions, there is a need for individuals to be assertive to maintain their self-esteem, but not to be aggressive and weaken the self-esteem of others.

The easiest way to distinguish assertiveness is to see it as a middle position between diffidence and aggression. Diffident people allow themselves to be trodden on, being anxious not to offend. They will feel badly about this behaviour, but will internalize the feeling as part of the diffident façade that is to be presented. Aggressive people express their feelings, which are of anger or outrage, in ways that offend or antagonize the people they are dealing with. Assertive people express their feelings, but in ways that are socially acceptable and that do not make them feel guilty.

One of the great attractions about assertiveness training is that it works! The methods are extremely practical and the majority of people who take courses find them of genuine value. Assertiveness *can* be learned. There are no assertive people, only people who have learned how to assert themselves.

Self-confidence

Each of us develops a self-estimate based on what others say about us and on our own assessment of how we measure up to the norms of the society of which we are a part. Poor self-estimate comes from concentrating more on our failures than our successes, so that we become preoccupied with what we cannot do (or think we cannot do) rather than what we can.

Self-estimate is improved by the drill of rehearsing in one's mind a list of things that are self-enhancing: 'I am friendly; I did well at school; I am accurate at calculations; I can make people laugh.' These then can squeeze out thoughts like 'I am fat; I am ugly; I do not express myself well; I am a mess.' Preoccupation with our failures can be self-fulfilling, so the shy person who retreats from friendly overtures will probably be judged as stand-offish or disdainful. Concentrating on and amplifying what is good about yourself can also be self-fulfilling.

Non-verbal and verbal clues		
Diffidence	*Assertion*	*Aggression*
Moving from one foot to another	Firm, comfortable stance	Leaning forward stiffly
Backing away from other person	Orienting towards other person	Moving against other person
Wringing hands	Hands relaxed	Clenched fists
Eyes averted or cast down	Eye contact with other person	Glaring, without expression
Voice hesitant or apologetic	Voice steady and clear	Voice staccato and overbearing
Tentative statements: I wonder/would you mind/maybe	Firm statements: I will/ I feel/I know/I want	Threats: I'm warning you/ you'd better
Negative statements: It doesn't matter/ never mind	Emphatic statements: What do you think/ can you help?	Critical statements: This won't do/It's not good enough
Fillers: You know/er/well now/ right	Cooperative words: Let's/what can we do/ how can we?	Sarcasm: You've got to be joking/ what makes you think …

Thought stopping

Self-confidence is undermined by negative thinking, both about yourself generally and in particular situations. Thought stopping is the process of reducing the impact of these negatives by working through a series of challenges to the depressing idea. Here are two examples:

I must be liked or approved of by those around me most of the time.

- *Negative effects* Can lose in competitive situations; can give false reassurance to people who need corrective guidance; can be cheated; can resist being angry in situations where anger is needed.

- *Stoppers* Although it is pleasant to be popular, it is not necessary to be popular with everyone. Doing what you think is right, or needed, is usually better than simply reacting to the demands of others. Taking the side of someone can make you very popular with that person, even if it makes you unpopular with another.

I should never make mistakes.

- *Negative effects* Can defer action/can direct attention to detail at expense of main issues/can miss promotion prospects because of feeling unready to apply for challenging jobs.

- *Stoppers* Although it is satisfying to be perfect, it is not necessary. Being perfect would not make me a better person. Perfection is so difficult to achieve that the desire is seldom satisfied. If a thing is worth doing, it is worth doing badly. Making mistakes can be the best way of improving performance.

Working with other people

1. *Make it easy for other people to do what you want them to do*
   Give clear reasons, be sure of your case and ask the right person.

2. *Speak up clearly*
   Praise other people, protect your own position, give feedback and be willing to say no.

3. *Define problems and work at them*
   When you have difficulty in working with someone, define what the problem is, consider alternative definitions, decide which is correct and work at dealing with it.

4. *Recognize the feelings of others*
   You are not the only one with problems; neither are you the only one who could be right.

Your Management Action

Exercises

1. Describe diffident, assertive and aggressive behaviours in each of the following situations:
    (a) You have taken an important client to an expensive restaurant for dinner, but there is no trace of your reservation and several other people are waiting too.
    (b) A colleague has just grumbled about one of your staff members and you feel the comment to be unfair.
    (c) Your boss rings to say she would like to see you for a meeting in half an hour. You have urgent work to complete and feel that it should take precedence over her meeting.
2. List five aspects of negative thinking that tend to undermine your self-confidence and then list some thought stoppers to counteract them.

Further reading

Bolton, R. Chapters 8-11, 'Assertion Skills' in *People Skills*, Simon and Schuster, Brookvale, NSW, 1987.
Bower, S.A. and Bower, G.H. *Asserting Yourself: A Practical Guide for Positive Change*, Addison Wesley, Reading, Mass., 1976.
Kelley, C. *Assertion Training: A Facilitator's Guide*, University Associates, San Diego, Calif., 1979.

And finally . . .

Assertive behaviour is always helped by knowing the social system in which you are dealing. Very few people have the confidence to send food back to the kitchen when they are dining in an expensive restaurant for example, yet frequently waiters will be potential allies. They have loyalty to you, the customer, from whom they expect a tip, as well as to the restaurant in general and the chef in particular. Have you ever seen a waiter refuse to take an underdone steak back to the kitchen? Also consider the sweet trolley. This is completely under the control of the waiter, and not the chef. The waiter wants your approval in order to get a tip: they will always give you a second helping.

7 Problem-solving and decision-making

There are many different problems and decisions requiring the manager's attention. It is often the area of work the least easy to describe as it is difficult to observe. Problem-solving is rarely a spectacular or exciting activity, but it is the one that is ignored at the organization's peril. Success in decision-making can rarely be guaranteed but there is scope for improving our ability to avoid failure. It is an important part of management work whether done alone or, more usually, in conjunction with others.

Problems become apparent rather than popping up clearly defined. Information from different sources begins to form a pattern. Once the problem is recognized – and recognizing it early is one of the arts of managing – someone needs to deal with it, seeking further information, pondering upon it and defining it more clearly; then deciding between alternative ways of dealing with it.

Many decisions that managers have to make are limited in their intellectual component. The challenge is not what should be done but other questions such as: Who should decide? What will be the reactions of the team? How do we make it work? The clever part of decision-making is getting commitment from others to try to make something work. An elementary rule is that people will support that which they have helped to create, which suggests participation and consultation. However, not all decisions can be taken this way. Sometimes there is not sufficient time and someone needs to say firmly, 'We are going to do this.' Where decisions are going to be unpopular some aspects will require consultation whereas others need executive action. For example, it is helpful to schools that governors are responsible for deciding that children are suspended, after which the staff can consult with the parents about how best to manage this.

Decision-making is rarely a totally rational process. Emotion, power politics, the influence of others, individual values, the search for a satisfactory compromise, lack of time, the pressure of action – all these work against the manager following a systematic decision-making path. Logical process can help unblock a problem; so can creativity. Intuition is no substitute for information, but it can sometimes save the day in situations when information is limited, uncertainties abound, time is short and the penalties for getting it wrong are not severe.

Ways of reacting to a problem

- Dealing with it yourself
- Passing it on
- Taking advice
- Working party approach
- Total quality management techniques and processes (included in The British Standard, BS 5750)
- Quality circles
- Mathematical modelling
- Using consultants
- Ignoring it

The problem-solving process

Here is a straightforward problem-solving process adapted from Stoner, 1982.

Stage 1	Stage 2	Stage 3	Stage 4
Definition and diagnosis	Generating alternatives	Deciding between alternatives	Implementation
Define problem	Generate alternative solutions	Consider available resources	Check availability of resources
Test definition	Defer judgement	Evaluate alternatives	Check understanding of those involved
Specify appropriate solution		Select most appropriate	Implement
			Monitor

Crises, problems and opportunities

Mintzberg, (et al. 1976), distinguish between crises, problems and opportunities:

- *Crisis* a sudden unexpected event requiring immediate action.
- *Problem* there is warning and it becomes apparent gradually, through clues from various sources and is not initially clear-cut.
- *Opportunity* chance to do something created by a single event and often needing swift action.

A crisis may of course create an opportunity.

Aids to decision-making

- Check-list
- Decision trees
- Computerized decision support systems
- Good quality information
- Intuition

Example: Decision Trees

A decision tree is a means of displaying the flow of possible courses of action in the form of a branching network. A large decision is broken up into a series of smaller decisions which can be made more easily, by examining the expected monetary gain at each decision point. The value of the decision tree is that it encourages management to lay out familiar information in a manner which leads to systematic analysis, and consequently better decisions. The squares represent points at which decisions must be made; the circles represent different possible events or results of actions which are uncontrollable.

The expected monetary yield can be worked out first at decision point B for years 3–10, and second at decision point A for years 1–10, by multiplying the estimated yield of each outcome by its probabilities and deducting the amount invested. There are many detailed descriptions of the method of calculation in the literature. The decision tree illustrated below indicates that the best choice at decision point A is to invest £1.5m in new machinery. Further sophistication may be added by taking into account differences in the time of future earnings by using discounting techniques.

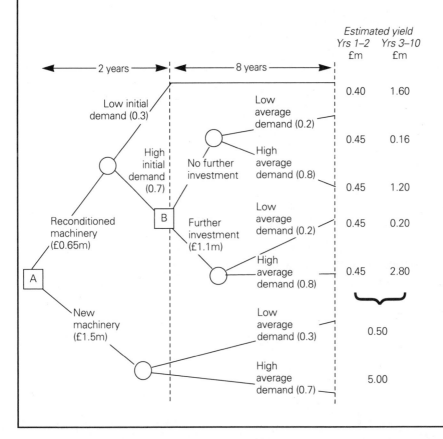

Your Management Action

Exercises

1. Think of specific examples from work to fit the Mintzberg definitions (section 7.2). Here are ours:
   - *Crisis* The canteen has burned down.
   - *Problem* There is poor morale among the staff.
   - *Opportunity* A tax law has changed.

2. Everyday decisions are often of the 'Yes, let's . . .' or 'No, I think not' type. How many small decisions did you make yesterday at work and at home? How many big decisions, affecting future action over six months, did you take?

3. Try jotting down factors you consider important to your family in the decision about the location of your next summer holiday.

Further reading

Adair, J. *Effective Decision Making*, Pan Books, London, 1985.
de Bono, E. *Tactics: The Art and Science of Success*, Fontana, London, 1986.
Kepner, O.H. and Tregoe, B.B. *The Rational Manager: A Systematic Approach to Problem Solving and Decision Making*, McGraw-Hill, Maidenhead, 1982.
Mintzberg, H.A., Raisingham, D. and Theoret, A. 'The Structure of Unstructured Decision Processes', *Administrative Science Quarterly*, June, 1976, pp. 246-75.
Stoner, J.A.F. *Management*, 2nd edn., Prentice-Hall, Englewood-Cliffs, N.J., 1982.

And finally . . .

There is little point in spending a lot of time and effort analysing a decision if the decision is not very important or you do not have the power to effect change. Factors to consider are:

- *Number of people involved*
- *Amount of money involved*
- *Length of commitment*
- *Flexibility once decision is made*
- *Certainty of the goals and assumptions made*
- *Quantifiability of the variables considered*
- *Human impact*
- *Environmental impact*
- *Finally, is this the right group of people to make the decision; do we have the power?*

8 Report-writing

Reports are written to be both read and acted upon. What the writer wants to say is not as important as what the reader wants to know and what the reader should do, so that reports are written not to interest nor even to inform, but to enable the reader to do something. This means that the action by the reader is the constant objective of the writer. Reports should be as brief as possible, but proposed action has to be thoroughly justified.

Before the writing begins there needs to be an outline, or *framework*. This will give a logical sequence to the writing and avoid risk of duplication, as well as presenting material early in the report that will be needed to justify points made later. The framework comes from analysing the message that is to be sent in terms of the action expected and then subdividing the components of that message into *logical groups*. The framework may be modified until the writer is convinced that it is satisfactory.

The groups should be put into *sections*, each dealing with a distinct aspect of the report material. The titles of these sections should not confuse the reader. 'Which way now?', for example, is unhelpful as it poses a question without giving any clue of the answer.

The *paragraph* is a unit of thought in the writing, dealing with a single topic or idea, and good paragraphing will ensure the material is read:

> Paragraphing is a matter of the eye. A reader will address himself more readily to his task if he sees from the start that he will have breathing spaces from time to time than if what is before him looks like a marathon course. (Fowler, 1968, p. 435.)

The appropriate length of a paragraph varies with the material being written. Textbooks usually average 100–200 words, popular novels 60–75 and popular newspapers 30–40. Short paragraphs are easier for the reader, but reports will sometimes require detailed argument involving greater length. It is wise to keep the average under 100 words, if possible.

The main difficulty in writing *sentences* is either that they are too long or that they set up expectations that are not realized. Overlong sentences come about through adding on extra clauses and qualifications. Setting up expectations that are not realized comes from inferring what is to come in the sentence, then moving on to a qualifying clause without returning to the original thought.

Report writer's check-list

1. Before writing
   (a)   What action do you expect from this report?
   (b)   Who will read it?
   (c)   How short can it be?

2. Outline
   (a)   What precisely is the topic of the report?
   (b)   How many components are there?
   (c)   How can those best be grouped?
   (d)   How are the components brought into sections?
   (e)   Do the titles inform the reader?
   (f)   Will the report, as outlined, produce the action specified in 1(a) above?

3. Writing the report
   (a)   Is the average paragraph length less than 100 words?
   (b)   Have you used more words than are needed?
   (c)   Have you used words that are precise and concrete rather than words that are vague and abstract?
   (d)   Have you any superfluous adverbs, adjectives and round-about phrases?
   (e)   Have you shown the source of any facts quoted?
   (f)   Are any of the sentences too long?

4. Revising the report
   (a)   Will the report, as written, produce the action specified in 1(a)?
   (b)   Is anything missing?
   (c)   Are any calculations accurate?
   (d)   Are the recommendations clear and justified?
   (e)   Is the choice between alternatives clear?
   (f)   Is any part of the report likely to cause offence to anyone? If so, can that be avoided?
   (g)   What objections do you expect to the recommendations, and how will you deal with them?
   (h)   Can any of the possible objections be prevented by rewriting part of the report?

5. Final presentation
   (a)   Is the typing perfect and without spelling mistakes?
   (b)   Are all the pages numbered?
   (c)   Are abbreviations and symbols used consistently throughout?
   (d)   Does the general appearance of the report encourage the reader to read it?
   (e)   Is there a single page summary of proposals?
   (f)   Is the report being distributed to all the appropriate people?
   (g)   If the report is confidential, is that indicated on the report and ensured by the method of distribution?

Some problems in writing

1. **Active and passive voice** The active voice is more direct and vigorous than the passive, so 'the roof leaks when it rains' is better than 'leaking is caused when the roof is rained on'

2. **Cant** describes phrases that have become meaningless through repetition, like 'by and large'. These are also known as clichés.

3. **Jargon** is vocabulary specific to a trade, profession or other group. It is useful shorthand for those who know, but bewildering to those who do not.

4. **Non sequitur** This is where the conclusion does not follow from the evidence, like the argument that computers will revolutionize management practice because they could.

5. **Syllepsis** is where metaphor is linked to the literal to make non-sense: 'She sat with her head in her hands and her eyes on the floor'.

6. **Tautology** is repeating what has already been said while implying extra meaning. 'Behaviour pattern' says no more than 'behaviour'; in the phrase '. . . not limited only to . . .' there is no need for 'only'.

Punctuation

- **Comma** makes a logical division within a sentence:
  - (a) to separate the subject from descriptive words or phrases, 'Charles, Prince of Wales, plays polo'.
  - (b) to separate clauses, 'if he scores, the crowd will cheer'.
  - (c) to separate items on a list, 'his parents, wife and children came to watch'.

- **Semi colon** links two sentences so closely related that a full stop would make too great a break, 'he didn't score; Jones did.'

- **Colon** separates an announcement from what is announced, 'the order of play is as follows:'

- **Apostrophe** indicates either a possessive, 'the team's performance' or a missing syllable in abbreviations, 'it's time for tea'.

Clichés to avoid

Afford an opportunity
Arguably
As it were
At the end of the day
At the present time
At this point in time
Be that as it may
For that matter
For the purpose of
Generally speaking
Give rise to
In a manner of speaking
In such a manner as to
In respect of
In the near future
In point of fact
Much of a muchness
No way
Owing to the fact that
Without fear or favour
Without fear of
  contradiction
With regard to

Your Management Action

Exercises

1. Reduce the second paragraph at the beginning of this chapter to improve its impact at the same time as reducing the number of words.

2. Review a report you have written using the points in section four of the report writer's check-list. How many alterations to the structure would you make?

3. Refer back to the first chapter of this book. Approximately what proportion of the sentences on a single page could be made shorter without losing any meaning?

4. When do you use a hyphen, brackets, inverted commas and an exclamation mark?

Further reading

Adair, J. *Training for Communication*, Gower, Aldershot, 1978.
Fowler, H.W. *Modern English Usage*, 2nd edn., Oxford University Press, Oxford, 1968.
Mayerson, E.W. *Shoptalk*. Saunders, Philadelphia, Pa., 1979.
The Oxford Dictionary for Writers and Editors, Clarendon Press, Oxford, 1981.

And finally . . .

It is always possible to trim out what is not necessary, as suggested in these last few pages, but there remains the need for some style to the writing. The reader needs not only accurate writing, but also a rhythm in the writing that makes it comfortable to read. Sometimes the bare, plain facts do not speak for themselves and the reader has to be persuaded to a point of view.

9 Reading

Many managers grumble about the amount of reading involved in their jobs. It is one of the duties that many feel impedes their progress in getting on with the 'real' work. This does not mean that all managers need to be able to read everything more quickly, but they need to be able to read effectively. The first step is to distinguish the types of reading that are involved.

First is reading for *identification*. Is the material to be thrown away as unimportant, filed against a possible future need, passed on to someone else, or kept to be read by the recipient? The reader will be looking mainly for the source and topic of the material to make this judgement. Second is reading for *information*, where the reader will be looking for the message in the writing: the request being made, the cost of the proposal, the date of the meeting or whatever specific piece of information is sought. This requirement produces the interest in reports that have the summary of proposals on a single sheet of paper. Sometimes the material will then be passed on to someone else, sometimes it will be kept for more careful study and sometimes it will be thrown away.

Reading for identification and reading for information are activities where speed and selectivity of the reader are valuable attributes. The next type is reading for understanding, where speed can be a hindrance. Now the reader is looking not for the message or 'the bottom line' but the reasoning that has led to the proposals and the evidence that is presented to support the argument. An example would be a tender for building work to be carried out. The reader would look first for identification and information: the source of the tender and its price. In moving on to understand the detail, a check would be made of what was included and what excluded, what materials were to be used, how long the work was to take, how payment was required and so forth. Sometimes this process takes on aspects of creative imagination where the reader looks for inferences. Readers of job references, for instance, frequently believe that they can discern hidden messages that are written between the lines, and those assessing competing business tenders look for indications of enthusiasm and determination among those submitting tenders.

A fourth type of reading is for criticism: looking for weaknesses or inconsistencies in what is written. This requires very detailed and careful examination of what is presented, with possible flaws mulled over and probably discussed with colleagues. This is found sometimes in the review of submitted tenders, so that queries can be put to the potential supplier with a view to re-submission. It is found in the drafting and negotiating of agreements and in proposals for commercial amalgamations.

Although it is generally true that most managers could read more quickly without losing effectiveness at any level, quicker reading could be an advantage to those reading for identification and information while being a handicap to those reading for understanding or criticism.

Drill for reading for identification

1.	Who is it from?	1.	Throw away
2.	Who (else) is it to?	*Alternative* 2.	File
3.	What is it about?	*actions:* 3.	Pass to . . .
4.	How important is it?	4.	Read

Drill for reading for information

1. Scan a full page at a time with a general left-right movement of the eyes, but 'pushing' down the centre of the page.

2. Use the opening of paragraphs as clues to significant information being imminent.

3. Pick out headings, illustrations, italics, bold type, underlinings, lists.

4. Check pages to scan by first checking contents list and index for clues to content.

5. Look for phrases that signal conclusions and summary statements:

> 'Therefore I believe . . .'
> 'The outcome of this is . . .'
> 'In contrast to this . . .'
> 'We suggest . . .'
> 'In conclusion . . .'

Preparing to read for understanding

1. *Decide how much you are going to read at a session and stop when you have done it.* This will assist both your understanding and your recall by giving you the satisfaction of fulfilling the contract you have made with yourself. When reading for understanding it can be unhelpful to read up to an immovable deadline, such as when your train reaches its destination, as you may be obliged to stop just before the penny drops.

2. *Review what you already know about the subject.* Either run the thoughts through your mind, check notes you have made previously or get a quick briefing from a colleague. If the material is completely new, it may be helpful to check in a reference book, such as looking up salient facts about the economy of a country before reading a market research report on prospects for doing business there. This provides a framework for the reading.

3. *Read with a purpose.* Decide why you are reading the material and set yourself a short list of questions that you want answered.

Reading for understanding

1. *Make notes* This makes your reading active, as you have to decide what to note and what not to note. The easiest way of doing this is with a pencil to underline phrases, make marks in the margin and scribble queries. A development of this is to use a text highlighter pen, very selectively, however, in order not to defeat the object of the exercise. If you write out notes on a separate sheet of paper, you are developing both understanding and recall as you are giving yourself the task both of deciding what material to select and then summarizing it in your own words.

   Taking a photocopy is no substitute for understanding.

2. *Review your notes* See if the marginal queries you pencilled in the first time have been resolved by your later reading. Have you missed an important feature that you did not appreciate until your first reading was complete? If there is anything you still do not understand, how can you resolve it? Do your notes make sense? Are there gaps?

Reading for criticism

1. What does not make sense?

2. What conclusions are not convincingly supported by argument and facts?

3. Where is evidence used to produce a conclusion when a different conclusion is equally, or more, feasible?

4. Are any facts incorrect or out of date?

Tips for reading more quickly

1. *Avoid vocalizing,* i.e. silently speaking the words as they are read. This reduces reading speed to speaking speed; speed will increase if the habit can be broken. Keep the lips shut tight and concentrate on not sounding the words.

2. *Reduce the number of fixations,* which is the number of times the eyes stop when scanning a line of type. Practise fixing on two words at a time, then three words and four words.

3. *Use a cursor,* which is a finger, a pencil or a piece of card, that you move along the line of type and down the page in front of the eyes. It focuses the eyes and leads them to move more quickly and more smoothly. This method is invariably used by people adding a column of figures but seldom used for the equally useful purpose of increasing reading speed.

Your Management Action

Exercises

1. Using a pencil as a cursor, read the first page of Chapter 11, taking a note of the time it takes you. Do that before reading any further on this page.

    *   How long did it take? If it took more than two minutes, you could certainly increase your speed.
    *   How many characteristics of Type A managers can you recall?
    *   How many of Smith's six major sources of stress can you recall? If you recall fewer than four in answer to the first question and fewer than five in answer to the second, your comprehension is below average. If this is associated with a reading speed of less than 90 seconds, you are probably reading too fast.

2. Re-read the opening chapter using the suggestions on the previous page regarding reading for understanding. In the same way, read two consecutive pages of your daily newspaper for information, followed by a leader for criticism.

Further reading

Buzan, T. *Use Your Head*, 2nd edn, BBC Publications, London, 1982.
De Leeuw, M. and E. *Read Better, Read Faster*, Penguin, Harmondsworth, 1965.

And finally . . .

Reading maketh a full man; conference a ready man; and writing an exact man.
(Francis Bacon, 1561-1626)

Reading is to the mind what exercise is to the body.
(Richard Steele, 1672-1729)

Education has produced a vast population able to read but unable to distinguish what is worth reading.
(G.M. Trevelyan, 1876-1961)

10   Presentation

Most managers have to make short speeches or presentations that are intended to increase the knowledge and understanding of a group of people, such as on a training course or at a sales convention. Few are good at it and many are terrified. It is the widespread fear of speaking in public that gives such power to those who seem to have conquered the fear. Considerable self-confidence comes to those who can cope with something that daunts most people they know.

Success in 'putting it over' lies not in transmitting a clear message, but in getting that message received and understood. There may be many different receivers, all of whom have to be kept switched on and tuned in by the speaker, with much less opportunity for feedback than there is in a conversation or small group discussion. The response and level of understanding will vary widely between different members of the audience. This can be illustrated by examples from entertainment: the most personable and popular of popular singers will never induce *all* members of the audience to reach a state of ecstasy; some will sit silent or inattentive. Even the comedian, getting a steadily rising level of laughter from the audience with every succeeding joke, will never make all the audience laugh.

The speaker in the lecture room, at the shareholders' meeting or at the sales conference will never get everyone's attention, but still needs to win over as many members of the audience as possible. As with other performances there is scope for preparation, rehearsal and careful manipulation of the physical environment to achieve the maximum effect.

The material for the presentation needs to be organized around a small number of *key thoughts* or *ideas*. There will probably be no more than three or four and they are what the speaker is trying to plant in the minds of the audience: not facts, which are inert, but the ideas which facts may well illustrate and clarify. The *fact* that England are 178 all out just after tea on the first day of a Test match is only an illustration of the familiar *idea* that yet another Test match is about to be lost.

The ideas in a presentation can be usefully linked together by a device that will help audience members to remember them and to grasp their interdependence. One method is to set them in a story. If the story is recalled the thoughts are recalled with it, as they are integral to the structure. Another method is to use key words to identify the points that are being made, especially if they have an alliterative or mnemonic feature, like 'Plans, Programmes and Profits'.

Facts, by creating impact, keep together the framework of ideas that the speaker has assembled. They clarify and give significance to what is being said, but they must be used sparingly, so that there are just enough to illustrate, but not enough to overwhelm the audience.

Check the room

1. *Have the right number of seats.* Too many will tend to scatter the members of the audience making it harder for the speaker to get them to behave like an audience rather than a collection of individuals.

2. *Speak from the right place.* Make sure there is somewhere to put your notes, no distracting background behind you (watch out for murals, stained glass windows, blackboards with writing on them, charts or windows).

3. *Check the equipment.* If using an overhead projector, make sure you know how to switch on and off and focus, make sure your prepared acetates can be read from the back of the room. Move the screen if necessary. After you have moved everything round, make sure the bulb still works and that the acetates are in the right order. Work out how to use the microphone.

Organize your material

The *introduction* is to:

*   set up rapport with the audience.
*   answer the unspoken question, 'Is it going to be worth listening?'
*   explain the framework of what is to come.

The *substance* is to convey the message using:

*   key thoughts or ideas
*   facts to illustrate
*   (with great care) humour

The *conclusion* is to:

*   reiterate and confirm.
*   integrate.
*   say what happens next.

Humour

Humour is valuable but dangerous. Use it only if you can be funny. If there is no response: stop.

Never risk humour that someone might regard as being in bad taste. Use it to illustrate, but never to distract; the listeners must recall your message, not the irrelevant funny story. Remember that people recall the jokes more clearly than any other part of the presentation.

Avoiding stage-fright

Few people avoid stage-fright. This releases adrenalin and is necessary for a vivid presentation. Too much stage-fright is disastrous: you have only the sympathy of the audience to fall back on. Reduce it by deliberately relaxing in the fifteen minutes before starting. Move more slowly than usual; consciously relax different muscles, especially by smiling. Breathe in to a steady count of three and out to an equally steady count of nine; in to four and out to twelve; in to five and out to fifteen and so on.

Using notes

Few people speak effectively without notes, which provide discipline, prevent omissions and limit the tendency to ramble. There are two kinds of notes.

1. *Headlines* are probably the most common, with main points underlined and facts listed beneath. Here is an example taken from the notes of a sales manager addressing a sales conference.

Points	Facts				Quotes, etc.
	Period	Us	Co.A	Others	
1. Our market share has declined over the last year	J-M	27%	22%	51%	(a) Comment by JB at advertising agency
	A-J	24%	26%	50%	
	J-S	25%	25%	50%	(b) Story from customer Z
	O-D	22%	27%	51%	
2. Not due to production difficulties	(a) No stoppages in period (b) Production has risen 3% (c) Customer complaints on quality down				Questions from works convener at production committee

2. The *script* enables the speaker to prepare the exact wording, phrases and pauses to achieve the greatest effect. The script will benefit from some marking that will help you to find your place again as your eyes constantly flick from the page to the audience and back again. This can be achieved by underlining or by using a highlighter. Another method of organizing a script is to use a form of blank verse. Here is an example of how a chaplain used this method not only to help him find his place, but also to give cues for pauses and emphasis.

It is not easy to live out your life day after day
and week after week
and year after year in a subordinate position,
while somebody else gets the notice
the publicity
the attention
the credit
the praise
the spotlight
and perhaps the reward

Getting them to listen

1. Speak so they can all hear
2. Look at the audience
3. Vary your tone
4. Don't gabble
5. Stand up straight
6. Be keen

Enthusiasm is contagious. If a speaker wants to convince, he has to believe in the issue himself. His belief helps to get the message across. There is a difference between 'We have to do something about wasted materials' said as the speaker picks lint off his trousers, scans the horizon, stifles a yawn, or scratches his head, and 'We have to do something about wasted materials' said with inflection, pausing, direct eye contact and an erect posture.

(Mayerson, 1979, p.184).

Your Management Action

Exercises

1. The next time you listen to a presentation or a speech given by someone else, study the arrangement of the room and decide how you would have arranged things differently if you had been the speaker. Why would you have made the changes? What would have been their effect?

2. Obtain from your library a book or audio cassette of speeches made by an effective orator, such as David Lloyd George, Winston Churchill, Billy Graham, John Kennedy or Martin Luther King. What lessons can you learn from how they planned their material?

3. Prepare a five-minute speech on one of these topics:
    *   Walking
    *   Gardening
    *   Your favourite sport
    *   Your hobby

Deliver the speech in an empty room and record it. Play it back several times, making critical notes of energy level, voice, pace and pauses, then deliver and record the speech again.
    *   In what ways is it better?
    *   In what ways not as good?
    *   What have you learned about the way you speak?
    *   What can you still improve?

Further reading

Bell, G. *Speaking and Business Presentations*, Heinemann, London, 1989.
Marks, W. *How to Give a Speech*, IPM, London, 1980.
Marshall, P. *Mr Jones, Meet the Master*, Peter Davies, London, 1954.
Mayerson, E.W. *Shoptalk*, Saunders, Philadelphia, Pa., 1979.

And finally . . .

Don't: *walk about all the time, draw elaborate patterns with the toe of your shoe in the imaginary dust on the floor, play constantly with your rings or bracelets, constantly take your glasses off.*

11   Managing stress

Managers often complain of having stressful jobs or stressful days at work. To be stressed has become almost a badge of status and importance in some circles.

What do we mean by stress? Stress is a demand made on our physical or mental energy. Where this is felt as excessive it is experienced as stressful and may lead to stress related physiological symptoms. The first symptoms may be irritability, excessive drinking, depression, raised blood pressure, headaches and chest pains. These can lead ultimately to diseases such as ulcers, coronary heart disease and mental illness. This definition implies that people will experience stress in different circumstances and some are able to cope better than others. One distinction that has been made is between type A people and type B. Type A are coronary prone and characterized by excessive competitiveness, alertness, irritability, feelings of responsibility and completely involved with their work. Type B are calmer characters, at less risk of suffering coronary heart disease. Although the clinical evidence for this distinction is debatable, we can all recognize ourselves and those we work with as tending towards type A or B. A useful point to note is that what is stressful to one person may not be to another, because we have different personalities, expertise and abilities.

Smith *et al. (1982)* identify six major sources of stress.

1. Every job has some aspects which someone, sometime, will find a source of stress. There can be too much to do, too little, or the work may be too difficult.

2. Managers may be uncertain about what to do, or they may have conflicting demands made upon them. Where the job involves responsibility for people this uncertainty is likely to increase and consequently lead to more stress.

3. The nature of relations at work can be stressful, particularly where there is mistrust.

4. Managers may experience stress because of their career prospects. This can be either through lack of job security or feeling that their status is unsuitable; both under-promotion and over-promotion can be sources of pressure.

5. The organizational climate can inhibit an individual's freedom and personal control. The more participation is permitted the less stress is felt.

6. A suitable balance between work and life outside the organization can be difficult to achieve. Pressure can come from the conflict of demands or crises. How to distribute time and commitment between home and work without the problems from one overflowing and creating problems in the other can become stressful.

Dealing with the sources of stress

1. **In the job**
    Short-term stress can be stimulating. Try to get the problem out of the way as soon as possible. Decide your priorities and stick to them.
    Long-term stress What are you doing that could be done by someone else? Are you treating everything with equal importance? Is this appropriate? Have you acquired new responsibilities without discarding some of the previous ones? Are you still doing your old job? What about discussing your job description with your boss or colleagues?

2. **Uncertainty and conflicting demands**
    Ask for clarification from the boss. Try the assertiveness techniques described in Chapter 6. The job is yours and you probably have more control over it than you think. Start by thinking about the choices open to you as described in Chapter 3. Set down your own goals using goal planning, as in Chapter 24.

3. **Poor working relationship with a colleague**
    If the difficulty is caused because the two of you have different goals, try to appreciate the other point of view and see if you can do some mutual goal-setting. Alternatively, the problem may be caused by a misunderstanding that you need to root out.

4. **Career prospects**
    The management ethic includes the idea of always going 'up', so that you may be classed as a failure if you are not seeking and gaining promotion. But what lifestyle suits you best? In any hierarchy there are more middle managers than senior managers, so do you want to gain your satisfaction from doing well the job you have rather than looking for another? More seniority seldom makes a person more secure in their job.

5. **Organizational climate**
    Is the climate as prohibitive as you think? Or is it an excellent excuse? What happens if you do try? Can you change it? Would another organization be any better?

Stability zones

We can cope with a lot of change, pressure, complexity and confusion if at least one area of our lives is relatively stable. Toffler *(1970)* suggested these stability zones were all-important. The main kinds of stability zones are: ideas, places, people and organizations. We all need security in at least one of these. Working out where your stability zones are and maintaining them helps to cope with stress in other areas.

Relaxation

- Sit or lie down comfortably, close your eyes and concentrate on relaxing.
- Starting at the top of your head feel each part of your body relax and get heavier.
- When the head feels heavy concentrate on the eyelids, mouth, chin, left hand, arm and so on down the body.
- Breathe through your nose and listen to your own breathing. It will get slower and slower.
- Try doing this every day starting with 10 minutes and working up to 20 minutes.

There are various techniques and courses run on relaxation. Yoga and meditation are well known. Bio-feedback techniques tell you when the pulse rate or breathing are reduced. Tapes that instruct you to relax might be worth a try.

Various other strategies

- *Excercise* Physical exercise uses the adrenalin that stress produces in the body.
- *Change of scene* A weekend away or a holiday can distract from the sources of stress. Cynics maintain this is the main purpose of training courses!
- *Life-planning* What do you want out of life? At home, at work, in your free time?
- *Therapy and self-help groups* Any group that listens and treats us seriously as individuals will provide a stability zone to help us cope with stress.
- *The spouse or close friends* Invaluable for listening and putting things into perspective.

Your Management Action

Exercises

1. Justify to your employing organization why they should pay for you to go on a skiing holiday rather than a week's management training course costing the same.

2. What are your stability zones? What have you done to cultivate and maintain them this week?

Further reading

Beynon, H. *Working for Ford*, Penguin, Harmondsworth, 1973.
Cooper, C.L. and R.D., Eaton, L.H. *Living with Stress*, Penguin, Harmondsworth, 1988.
Pedler, M., Burgoyne, J. and Boydell, T. *A Manager's Guide to Self Development*, McGraw-Hill, Maidenhead, 2nd edn., 1986.
Smith, M., Beck, J., Cooper, C.L., Cox, C., Ottaway, D. and Talbot, R. *Introducing Organisational Behaviour*, Macmillan, London, 1982.
Stewart, R. *Choices for Managers*, McGraw-Hill, Maidenhead, 1982.
Toffler, A. *Future Shock*, Pan, London, 1970.

And finally . . .

However stressed a manager may feel it is a sobering thought that those lower in the hierarchy show more symptoms of stress than those higher up the ladder.

> *It's a relief when you get off the moving line. It's such a tremendous relief. I can't put it into words. When you're on the line it's on top of you all the time. You may feel ill, not one hundred per cent, but the line will be one hundred per cent.*
>
> *(Benyon, 1973, p. 118)*

Part B

Managing in the organization

12 Organization structure

Organization is the start of the process that makes people working together achieve what they cannot do individually. It is the distribution of power to make decisions and get things done, choosing which skills and expertise to group together, and deciding how working groups interconnect and communicate. Because organization limits individual freedom of action, people will often fight against it, trying to 'short circuit the system' or 'cut through the red tape'. The harder you work at getting the organization right for your situation, the less will be the fighting against it; but it must be appropriate to your business and the people who are involved. Overleaf we describe four types of organization structure. Although seldom found in pure form, they represent features that will be found in most businesses.

Organizing begins with labelling. Every organization member has a label explaining the content and boundaries of her or his job. The employee needs the label to answer questions like 'What do you want me to do?' 'How much scope have I got?' 'Where does my job fit in with everyone else's?' and (perhaps) 'How and when can I get promoted?' There are also questions about other people's labels, 'Who do I ask about . . .?' 'Who is in charge?' 'Who else do I work with?' Without good labelling there is uncertainty and inefficiency. Often the label is no more than a job title, which is enough when it is explicit and widely understood, like electrician or cook, but vague titles usually require a job description to make clear the duties and, especially, the boundaries of jobs.

The second step is grouping, deciding the membership of various working groups and how their activities interconnect. What skills and functions should be grouped together into different departments and divisions? What grouping will lead to effective collaboration rather than dissatisfaction and attempts to beat the system?

The scope of decisons to be made by individuals will be defined by their labels or by their positions in the groupings, but some decisions are made collectively by decision-making complexes (DMCs). These may be committees, councils, teams or groups.

The fourth feature is operating procedures: the ways in which decisions are implemented, and the standard ways of getting things done in the organization. How are purchase orders authorized? When new employees join the company, how are they included on the payroll?

All of these can lead to inefficiency and frustration when they go wrong and they are then difficult to put right. The usual method is 're-organization' which involves changing labels and groupings, often in a panic and seldom including attention to DMCs and procedures. These moves may have more to do with assertions of power and problems of status than with problems of organization. Balancing the power and influence of personalities is important, but it is not a sufficient principle on which to base all organizational decisions.

Types of organization

The **entrepreneurial** form emphasizes power at the centre. One person or small group is so dominant that all power stems from there, all decisions are made in the light of central expectations and all people in the organization mirror central behaviour. This sort of strong centralization is found often where there is a need to move fast and to take major decisions needing flair and judgement rather than a measured weighing of alternatives.

Few decisions are taken collectively, there is little dependence on procedures, and actions stem from getting the approval of key figures, with decisions often based on precedent. This form is how most organizations begin life, with the logic of depending on the special knowledge of the founder who made the business possible. In large, functional undertakings it is usually found in areas like marketing, among people who enjoy individual power, risk and competition.

The **bureaucratic** form groups jobs by some common feature, like function or location, and groups them in a hierarchy of responsibility to distribute power among members of the organization. Emphasis is on role rather than flair and judgement. In stable situations bureaucracy makes possible economies of scale and the benefits of job specialization. It is seldom flexible enough to be suitable for volatile situations.

Action stems from consistent use of procedures, often incorporating decision-making by committee to ensure thorough consideration of issues and to guard against corruption. This form tends to be liked by those seeking clearly-defined duties and responsibilities.

The **matrix** form has been developed to overcome some of the shortcomings of the first two. A conventional hierarchy has a second set of hierarchical connections laid over the first, and running at right angles to it. The vertical lines are of function, but the horizontal lines link people from different areas to share full responsibility for a particular project requiring skills from each function, making each member a functional plenipotentiary for the duration of the project.

Action is based on expertise in a specific context and it can be a popular form for those wanting not only to deploy their skills but also to enjoy a sense of responsibility and contribution. Although first used to cope with the complex organizational demands of high technology, it has lost favour because it tends to cause costly support services and unwieldly administration.

The **independence** form is a type of non-organization. Instead of putting the contributions of people together so that the sum is greater than the parts, the organization is no more than a support system enabling individuals to perform.

Many professional practices and consultants work in this way, so that barristers' chambers and doctors' clinics provide the facilities for them to work separately rather than together. The form is attractive to those who are independently-minded and confident of their ability to be individually successful. Although it has been regarded as unsuitable for most types of job, the growing number of freelance specialists and others working from home has increased interest in this form.

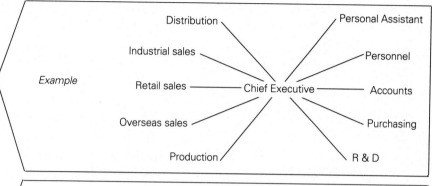

Example

- Distribution
- Industrial sales
- Retail sales ——— Chief Executive
- Overseas sales
- Production
- Personal Assistant
- Personnel
- Accounts
- Purchasing
- R & D

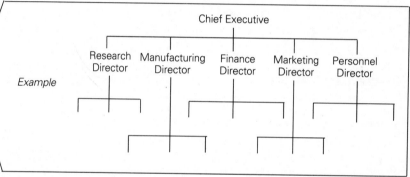

Example

Chief Executive

- Research Director
- Manufacturing Director
- Finance Director
- Marketing Director
- Personnel Director

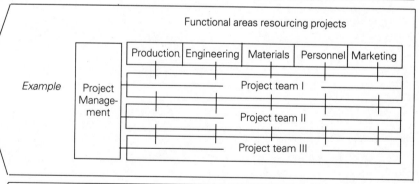

Example

Functional areas resourcing projects

Project Management

Production	Engineering	Materials	Personnel	Marketing

Project team I

Project team II

Project team III

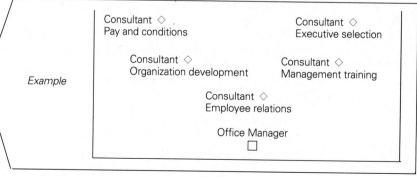

Example

Consultant ◇
Pay and conditions

Consultant ◇
Executive selection

Consultant ◇
Organization development

Consultant ◇
Management training

Consultant ◇
Employee relations

Office Manager
□

Your Management Action

Exercises

1. For the organizational situations listed below, which of the four forms of organization would you regard as most suitable?
    (a) The flight deck of a passenger aircraft
    (b) Developing sophisticated weaponry to military specifications
    (c) The high street branch of a retail bank
    (d) A sales force
    (e) A school
    (f) An orchestra

2. How would you describe the emphasis in the organization of your present company?

3. Think of some jobs in your organization and decide how a change of label for them might improve efficiency.

4. In your organization, which DMCs should be replaced by individual decision makers and which decisions made by individuals would be better taken by DMCs?

Further reading

Child, J. *Organization*, 2nd edn, Harper and Row, London, 1984.
Fowler, A. 'Getting in on Organization Restructuring', *Personnel Management*, February, 1985, pp 24-7.
Handy, C.B. *Understanding Organizations*, 3rd edn, Penguin, Harmondsworth, 1985.
Leavitt, H.J., Dill, W.R. and Eyring, H.B. *The Organizational World*, Harcourt, Brace, Jovanovich, New York, 1973.
Peters, T. *Thriving on Chaos*, Pan Books, London, 1989.
Peters, T.J. and Waterman, R.H. *In Search of Excellence*, Harper and Row, London, 1982.

And finally . . .

Peters and Waterman point out the risk of regarding re-organizing as being all the required answer to cope with change:

> An organization chart is not a company, nor a new strategy an automatic answer to corporate grief. We all know this; but like as not, when trouble lurks, we call for a new strategy and probably re-organize. And when we re-organize, we usually stop at re-arranging the boxes on the chart. The odds are high that nothing much will change.
>
> (Peters and Waterman, 1982, p.3)

13   Organizational culture

Organizational culture is the characteristic spirit and belief of an organization, demonstrated, for example, in the conventions about how people should behave and treat each other, and the type of working relationships that should be developed. It is developed in all sorts of ways and is mostly taken for granted. Interest in culture has grown only recently, as a reaction against the more limited concern with structure that prevailed until the 1980s. Culture is the flesh on the bones of structure.

Corporate culture is an attempt to foster specific objectives in relation to behaviour and values. This entices customers to buy, it entices prospective employees to seek jobs and encourages them to feel commitment to the organization. This can be expressed and reinforced in various forms, such as a formal statement from the Chief Executive, or in comments like 'we don't do things that way here'. There is the logo, the stationery, the uniform: all part of the corporate image.

Managers have to understand what the prevailing culture in their organization is, how it ought to be changed, the extent to which it can be changed and how those changes may be made. They also need to recognize that the changes may be much harder and slower to make than most managers believe and most circumstances allow.

Culture is difficult because it is intangible – you cannot draw it like an organization chart. It is nonetheless real and powerful, so that the enthusiastic managers who unwittingly work counter-culturally will find that there is a metaphorical but solid brick wall against which they are beating their heads. Managers who pause to work out the nature of the culture in which they are operating can at last begin the process of change and influence the direction of the cultural evolution, because culture is living, growing and vital, able to strengthen and support the efforts of those who use it, as surely as it will frustrate the efforts of those who ignore it.

Organizational cultures are typically dominated by traditional male values of rationality, logic, competition and independence, rather than the traditional female values of emotional expression, intuition, caring and interdepen-dence (Marshall, *1984*). It is not necessary that organizational cultures should be biased in this way, but it seems that an organization has to be set up from scratch by women if it is to develop a different culture:

> 'Women . . . may not be properly represented at important levels of big corporations, but they are now doing remarkably well in the firms they have set up themselves. Here, they don't have to play the male game according to male rules. They are free to make up their own rules, make relationships rather than play games, run their businesses more on a basis of trust than of fear, cooperation rather than rivalry.
>
> (Moir and Jessel, *1989*, p.167)

National cultures

Geert Hofstede *(1980)* analysed 116,000 questionnaires administered to employees in 40 different countries and concluded that national cultures could be explained by four key factors.

1. *Power distance*   This measures the extent to which the less powerful members of a society accept the unequal distribution of power, centralization of authority and the exercise of autocratic leadership.

2. *Uncertainty avoidance*   The future is always unknown. Some societies socialize their members to accept this and take risks, while members of other societies have been socialized to be made anxious about uncertainty and to seek the security of law, religion or technology.

3. *Individualism*   The extent to which people desire to look after themselves and their family only. The opposite is collectivism which has a tight social framework, where people expect to have a wider social responsibility because others will in turn support them. Those of collectivist views believe they owe absolute loyalty to their society.

4. *Masculinity*   In a society where men are assertive and have dominant roles, these values permeate the whole of society and the organizations that make them up, so there is an emphasis on showing off, performing, making money and achieving something visible. Where there is a larger role for women, who are more service oriented with caring roles, values move towards concern for the environment, and putting the quality of relationships before the making of money.

Hofstede found some clear national cultural differences between nationalities. A sample of scores of the four criteria are shown below.

Criterion	High score	Low score
Power distance	Mexico	Austria
	Philippines	Denmark
	Venezuela	Israel
	Yugoslavia	New Zealand
Uncertainty avoidance	Belgium	Denmark
	Greece	Hong Kong
	Japan	Singapore
	Portugal	Sweden
Individualism	Australia	Colombia
	Canada	Pakistan
	Great Britain	Peru
	United States	Venezuela
Masculinity	Austria	Denmark
	Italy	Norway
	Japan	Sweden
	Venezuela	Yugoslavia

Developing organizational culture

Ed. Schein (1985) distinguishes between the primary (more effective) and secondary (less effective) mechanisms for the change and consolidation of organization cultures.

Primary mechanisms
(a) What leaders pay most attention to;
(b) How leaders react to crises and critical incidents;
(c) Role modelling, teaching and coaching by leaders;
(d) Criteria for allocating rewards and determining status; and
(e) Criteria for selection, promotion and termination.

Secondary mechanisms
(a) The organizational structure;
(b) Systems and procedures;
(c) Space, buildings and façades;
(d) Stories and legends about important events and people;
(e) Formal statements of philosophy and policy.

And a warning . . .

Culture is a liability where the shared values are not in agreement with those that will further the organization's effectiveness.

(Robbins, 1986, p. 436)

Your Management Action

Exercises

1. Identify three ways in which your organization shows a dominance of
    male values and three ways in which female values are dominant. What
    would be the effect on the success of the organization if female values
    were to spread further (specify how) or if male values were to spread
    further (specify how)?

2. Think of an organization of which you are or have been a member that
    had a strong leader. This may not necessarily have been an employing
    organization, but a school, youth club, dramatic society, campaigning
    group, or political party.
       Work out the extent to which the leader shaped the culture of the
    group. In what ways did the culture resist the leader's attempts to shape
    it? How were the shaping and the resistance manifested?

Further reading

Barham, K. and Rassam, C. *Shaping the Corporate Future*, Unwin Hyman,
    London, 1989.
Goffee, R. and Scase, R. *Women in Charge*, Allen and Unwin, London, 1985.
Hofstede, G. *Culture's Consequences*, Sage, Beverly Hills, Calif., 1980.
Marshall, J. *Women Managers: Travellers in a Male World*, Wiley, Chichester,
    1984.
Moir, A. and Jessel, D. *Brain Sex*, Michael Joseph, London, 1989.
Olins, W. *Corporate Identity*, Thames and Hudson, London, 1989.
Robbins, S.P. *Organizational Behavior*, Prentice-Hall, Englewood Cliffs,
    New Jersey, 1986.
Schein, E.H. *Organizational Culture and Leadership*, Jossey-Bass, San
    Francisco, Calif., 1985.

And finally . . .

*Culture is the passion for sweetness and light, and – what is more – the passion
for making them prevail.*
                                            (Matthew Arnold, 1822-1888)

When I hear anyone talk of culture, I reach for my revolver.
                                            (Hermann Goering, 1893-1946)

14 Corporate social responsibility

What goes on inside a business is affected by all sorts of things going on around it. We have already considered the way in which organizational culture depends largely on the cultural features of the surrounding society, but there are many other aspects of the interaction between the organization and its context.

First the organization is part of the *political system* of the nation in which it is set and the political realities which that system produces. The management of the business will alter drastically according to the policies of the government of the day and will be constrained by the legal system of the land. At one extreme a business can be dismantled or can require root and branch change in functioning as a result of nationalization, privatization, re-nationalization or other types of political initiative. At a different level one business may be bankrupted by a change of government policy, while others may be created as a result of that same change.

The viability of the government's policies will also crucially depend on what goes on inside the business. One widely held view for many years has been that the single most important cause of rising inflation is high pay settlements. Governments have used statutory control mechanisms like pay policy and have abandoned statutory mechanisms in favour of market solutions, yet inflation persists. The balance of payments is always a central element in the economic strategy of any government. A favourable balance may be aided by government action, but it is mainly commercial business that will increase, or fail to increase, their exports and imports.

The organization is also part of the *social system* in which it is set. If the values obtaining in that social system sustain the Protestant work ethic, or frequent industrial action, or 'inducements' paid to government employees to win contracts, or equal opportunity programmes, or high taxation, or national service, then the workings of the business have to fit within that system of constraints and opportunities. One of the hardest parts of working across national boundaries is coming to terms with the social conventions that operate.

The issues of *corporate social responsibility* are extensive and becoming more varied. There is a call for those with business expertise to become involved in the running of charities and public bodies like schools and parts of the health service, so that their expertise can be used outside the commercial sector. A more general involvement in the local community is advocated because of the economic dependence of the local community on the local employers. If there are problems of unemployment, it is employers who can provide the logical answer to those problems, even though they may need central or local government assistance. By far the most topical issue of social responsibility at present is concern for the environment.

Environmental issues

The environment is becoming an increasingly important issue for all types of business. There is increasing pressure on businesses to improve their environmental record on atmospheric and water pollution, storage and disposal of hazardous substances, energy conservation and similar matters. A report by the Institute of Business Ethics *(1990)* showed that over 30 per cent of the companies surveyed had introduced an environmental policy.

Among the benefits to organizations of 'going green' are (Crabb, *1990*):

- improved public and customer relations
- improved recruitment due to heightened sensitivity of potential recruits to environmental issues and consequent selectivity in employment approaches
- improved morale following the adoption of 'green' policies, such as healthy foods in the canteen and no-smoking rules.

A green audit

A directive under discussion by the European Council would require all companies to carry out an environmental audit. There is also increasing interest from trade unions in green issues; NALGO, TGWU and TUC are planning courses for union members on the environment. Many green questions are specific to the manufacturing processes of an individual business, but here are some general areas to question.

1. *Atmospheric or water pollution*   This can be reduced by trying to eliminate products and processes using substances such as CFCs, particularly in aerosols. In 1990 Shell was fined £1 million for polluting the River Mersey with oil – the highest penalty imposed by a British court for such an offence.
2. *Waste*   Careless dumping has caused considerable problems. Some progress is being made by more thoughtful disposal such as chemical treatment and landfill measures and the development of biodegradable packaging, as well as the recycling of aluminium, glass and paper.
3. *Energy*   More can probably be done in insulation and heating controls to preserve energy, as well as the myriad of small measures such as using time switches or encouraging staff to switch off lights when leaving a room. A few organizations now provide bicycles for staff use: the London Borough of Sutton pays the same mileage rates for bicycle use as for car use.
4. *Petrol*   Company cars can be converted to use lead-free petrol and can be fitted with catalytic convertors to reduce emissions. British Telecom has converted its fleet of 66,000 vehicles to run on unleaded petrol.

A riposte

Just to get you thinking, here is a counter argument, suggesting that social responsibility may *not* be a suitable topic for management interest.

We all have specialized roles and our competence is limited to them. The idea that managers should make decisions on issues of social responsibility is bizarre and in conflict with both their social role and their legal responsibilities, for these reasons:

1. Managers have to satisfy their shareholders. Pension funds, for instance, have to depend on reliable income from their investments. If a major bank cuts its dividend for the first time in 58 years as a result of ill-conceived investments in South American social experiments, that is failing to meet the reasonable expectations that stem from their prime reason for existence.

2. Managers have to satisfy their customers. If a major car manufacturer were to decide that all their production cars were to operate on lead-free petrol only, some customers would say that it is not for the manufacturer to decide: the customer should not be denied choice.

3. Managers have to provide an effective management service to their employees, to whom they have a greater responsibility than to the locality. If they neglect the boring business of running the factory because being a governor of the local primary school is novel and more interesting, they are abrogating their principal social responsibility.

4. Managers lack objectivity in social matters because of their concern with public relations. There is a great deal of commercial sponsorship of the arts. If *Pride and Prejudice* is staged at the local theatre, many companies would be delighted to sponsor it, as it is classical, wholesome, by a well-known author and an 'A'-level text. A modern play by an unknown author on the persecution of gay activists would be a very poor candidate for commercial sponsorship.

5. Managers' commercial imperatives override socially responsible preferences. Day nurseries were a popular and lauded 'socially responsible' initiative during the 1980s, but they began to close when young mothers were no longer so desperately needed in the workforce.

It is not for people in management positions to determine social priorities. They should respond to the law, to the social responsibility of their employees and to the market. That is the only way it will work. Otherwise our social priorities will become progressively overwhelmed by commercial considerations. That which is expedient will become good. That which is commercial will be funded.

Your Management Action

Exercises

1. Look round your office now and decide how you (not the company) can be more socially responsible in what you use, how you use it and what you waste.
2. Write a list of actions which the company could intitiate that would be socially responsible, and where you are in a position to influence the necessary decisions. Reduce the list to no more than three. Set yourself a target date for getting them started and make a note in your diary to check how successful you have been.
3. Answer the points made in 'A Riposte' above.

Further reading

Crabb, S. 'Has industry seen the green light?' *Personnel Management*, April, 1990, pp. 42-7.

Falconer, H. 'Courage of convictions', *Personnel Today*, July, 1990, pp. 22-3.

Institute of Business Ethics, *Ethics, Environment and the Company*, IBE, London, 1990.

Lowe, K. 'Made to measure but for whom?' *Personnel Today*, July, 1990, pp. 26-8.

Pocock, P. 'Is business ethics a contradiction in terms?' *Personnel Management*, November, 1989, pp. 60-3.

And finally . . .

ASDA, the retailers, ran a course in conjunction with the Nottingham Task Force and Clarendon College of Further Education for people who had been long-term unemployed. ASDA designed a course to meet their specific requirements. Potential recruits were identified by the Task Force and guaranteed an interview after training. The course initially dealt with practical information on job hunting, job applications and the retail business. The remainder of the course was based in-store under staff supervision. Over 70 long-term unemployed people were recruited to ASDA through this scheme (Lowe, 1990).

The Apex Trust deals with the rehabilitation of ex-offenders, working closely with employers. They recently set up a project offering work placements to prisoners. Training is provided by employers within prisons, together with placements on a day release basis (Falconer, 1990). Apex is also planning to launch a two-year pilot scheme which will include issuing fidelity bond insurance to employers to protect themselves against loss incurred through possible dishonest acts of employees. This will be available to employers who recruit ex-offenders, but who are not appropriately covered by their current insurance.

15 Dealing with problems of organization

Organizations may be over-managed through having too many people whose job is to coordinate and integrate the work of others. Well-meaning delegation can produce small packets of responsibility that slow down action because of the large number of people to be consulted and informed. This is especially a problem for those who see themselves as 'managed' rather than 'managing', because they see management as a confused collection of people, few of whom appear able to provide a clear decision or authoritative guidance. It is also a problem for senior managers, who feel distanced from the people engaged on the main tasks of the organization by a middle management jungle.

The *size* of the organization may be inappropriate to its mission. There has been much enthusiasm recently for making operational units smaller to avoid the problems of impersonality and alienation associated with large organizations. However, smaller is not always more beautiful; complex operations may need large numbers of people and specialist facilities to sustain them.

No organization can function without adapting to its *context*. This includes, obviously, the product market, fiscal policy and taxation. It is not always so obvious that the social context is equally important, especially the labour market.

Many organizational problems stem from job definition and rigidity. Those whose duties are precisely drawn are encouraged by that precision to view their range of activities as strictly delimited: 'that is not in my job description, so I will not do it'. This can be regarded as an uncooperative, obstructive attitude, but it is just as likely to be due to a concern not to encroach upon someone else's area of responsibility, or anticipation of reprimand for exceeding responsibilities. When job descriptions are less precise, there is the danger that important matters will be overlooked, because responsibility is not defined, and members of the organization will do whatever they want to do rather than what they should do.

It is important to ensure that decisions to be made by individuals are so made, and that those which need to be made collectively are remitted to the appropriate body with the requisite authority to act. Is it a decision that needs individual flair and judgement, with the subsequent personal accountability that will result, or is it a decision that needs collective wisdom and consent to aid its subsequent implementation?

In the next two pages we have some suggestions for dealing with problems like these, but we need to reiterate our earlier the comments about the importance of thoroughness. Getting the organization right and developing it to suit changing circumstances and changing personnel requires shrewd judgement and careful attention to details. It requires eternal vigilance also: organization is seldom 'right' for long.

The problem of over-management

A good indication of over-management lies in the steepness of the hierarchy; increasing the number of subordinates reporting to a single manager can flatten the hierarchy and reduce the problem.

1. How many tiers are there in the hierarchy? Can any of these be removed?

2. Can some of the jobs defined as management be redefined as specialist or professional, so that they are taken out of the management direct line without any loss of status?

3. How much can the autonomy of the managed be increased? The greater the autonomy, the less need for supervision and the larger the number of people to be the responsibility of one manager.

4. Can the amount of target-setting be increased, so that the duties of employees are defined by output as well as method? This, too, will increase the number of people who can be the responsibility of one manager.

5. Can members of the organization achieve social status by means other than their managerial rank? To a large extent the steepness of the hierarchy is a product of social pressure to improve career prospects and enhance status. If there are alternative sources of those rewards, the social pressure is reduced.

The problem of size

Organizations tend to become more bureaucratic as they grow, and also tend to steepen the hierarchy, with associated difficulties about morale among members distant from the centre. However, organizational growth does provide career growth and opportunities for changes of job among members.

1. Is there any part of the work of the organization that could safely be detached, either as a separate, autonomous organizational unit, or as a set of requirements placed on an external supplier? This could reduce organizational size, but are there potential problems that would outweigh the advantages, such as loss of control, security, etc?

2. Do you make the best use of consultants to avoid the need to increase the size of your organization, or are you in danger of becoming dependent on them?

3. Do you get the type of service you require from all your suppliers, or would you get better integration of some services by setting up your own specialist department within your own business?

4. In order to overcome the problems of low morale among organization members distant from the centre, are there ways in which operating units within the organization structure can be made more autonomous?

The problem of context

Strategic objectives can be more ambitious if the setting is buoyant, or competitive, and organization members will be more creative if the setting is changing and presenting challenges.

1. Does the way in which jobs are organized provide the range of opportunities, challenges and responsibility that general social developments are causing members of the organization to expect?
2. Are the various boundary roles in the organization set up in a way that provides the optimum interface between internal activities and the external context?

The problem of job rigidity

Apart from the problem of rigidity already mentioned, the main difficulty of job definition is where there is the possibility of overlap or omission.

1. Are there any activities within the organization where there is uncertainty about who has the responsibility? Can this uncertainty be usefully clarified?
2. Where there are job descriptions, do job holders regard them as a useful framework for their contribution, as a straitjacket limiting their scope, or as irrelevancies? If they are a straitjacket, can they be altered? If they are irrelevant, can they be thrown away?
3. Do job holders write their own job descriptions or have them written by someone else? If they are written by the job holders they are probably useful; if written by someone else they could be useless.

The problem of decisions

Decisions can go wrong because they are taken too hastily, or because they are taken too late and an opportunity has been missed. Much depends on how the matter requiring decision is presented to the decision maker(s).

1. Are collective decisions made on matters requiring a range of expertise, or where implementation of the decision may be difficult because of employee resistance? This type of decision normally should not be taken by an individual.
2. Are individual decisions made on matters that are straightforward, with policy precedents or procedural guidance, those needing very specialized experience or flair, and those matters on which individual accountability is important? This type of decision normally should not be taken collectively.
3. Does the organization have a convention whereby people are encouraged to decide quickly when a matter would be considered better at length?
4. Does the decision-making convention encourage prevarication?

Exercises

1. Sketch out your organization chart and check it for over-management.
    (a) Can any of the jobs where the title includes the word 'manager' have that element removed without a loss of status by the job holder and with an improvement to organizational efficiency?
    (b) Can you reduce the number of hierarchical levels?
    (c) Is there scope for increasing the autonomy of job holders?

If your answer is 'yes' to any of the above questions, sketch an improved organization chart and summarize the benefits it will provide.

2. Is your organization too big or too small? How can you move it towards a more appropriate size?

3. In what ways is your organization not properly attuned to the setting in which it operates?

4. To what extent does slack job definition need to be tightened up and to what extent is job definition too rigid?

5. Jot down 10 decisions that you can recall from the recent past that were dubious. Could any of them have been made better by different organization?

Further reading

Child, J. *Organization*, 2nd edn, Harper and Row, London, 1984.
(Chapter 3 is particularly appropriate to the question of over-management and the span of control.)

Khandwalla, P.N. *Design of Organisations*, Harcourt, Brace, Jovanovich, New York, 1977. (This book contains detailed and extensive suggestions about how to identify problems of organization.)

Pile, S. *The Book of Heroic Failures*, Routledge and Kegan Paul, London, 1979.

And finally . . .

A problem of organization:

In July 1978 Sir Peter Parker, Chairman of British Rail, set off to attend a meeting with Cumbria County Council. Delayed by traffic, he arrived at Crewe Station just as the train was leaving. He tore through the ticket barrier, waved a BR pass and leaped on. As the journey progressed, it dawned on him that far from being on the express to Carlisle, he was aboard the non-stopper for London. Eventually he persuaded the guard to throw a note wrapped round a coin out of the window as the train thundered through Tamworth Station in Staffordshire. It said, 'Please apologize to Cumbria Council and tell them I won't be able to make it.'

(Pile, 1979.)

16 Analysing your network of contacts

Managers spend a lot of time talking to other people. Who they talk to is important as it affects what influences are brought to bear on the decisions and actions that result from these conversations. Some contacts will be made because of the formal relations between job titles but a lot of contacts are the result of the manager's personal network of people. Another person doing the same job would have different contacts.

Thus organizational contacts can be described in two ways: *hierarchies* and *networks*. Hierarchies are characterized by the organization chart that outlines the formal relations between members of a particular organization. The chart tells us the formal distribution of power and authority, who reports to whom, the approved channels of communication, links between sections and also something of how the work is organized. This statement of the hierarchy takes us from the macro level of organization structure to the micro level of individual contacts within the organization.

Work by Kotter (1982) has demonstrated that individual managers will also have a network of contacts. He found that this was different from, but consistent with, the formal organization structure. Networks are co-operative relationships with people who can help you accomplish things. They are subordinates, peers, outsiders, the boss's boss, subordinate's subordinate or anyone on whom you are dependent to get things done. These networks are often large. Kotter's general managers' included hundreds or thousands of people, and every relationship is different. The network is for sharing ideas, information and resources. It gives particularly the horizontal link not prescribed in the organizational chart. Networks include 'knowing how the system works'.

Contacts are created and maintained by the whole range of interpersonal behaviours. Some will be personal friends made in previous jobs or at college. Others will be new contacts made because they are politically necessary. A manager's network is not the same as the old boy system. The difference is that the old boy system is protecting the self-interest of a limited few whereas the network is widespread and essential to get things done.

This chapter is rather different from the others. It consists of an exercise designed to help you bring together ideas from several other chapters and to analyse how they affect you and your job. We ask you to look at both the formal and informal contacts at work and analyse whether they need improving. This interpersonal contact is the main theme of much of this book. Some chapters, such as 12, 20, 25 and 36, deal with why it is important to make the contact, while others, for example Chapters 5, 38, and 45, help with how to make the contact more effective.

The organization chart

Draw a personal organization chart, with yourself at the centre, using ☐ to indicate job positions and showing the names of those currently holding those posts. The chart should include formal relations you have inside and outside the organization. The circle represents the organization boundary. On the right is an example of a typical organization chart.

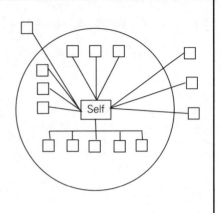

The network of contacts

On a second chart list all the individuals or groups who can influence how effective you are in your job, but with whom you do not have a formal working relationship included in the first chart. Give both names and positions. The drawing, which may look something like the one on the right, will illustrate your informal network.

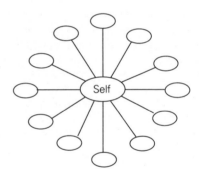

Evaluating the network of contacts

- Use the form opposite to rank the contacts, formal and informal, in their order of importance to you in getting your job done effectively.

- Rate each contact on a scale between –3 and +3, according to how helpful the person is to you.

- What can be done to improve communication with those you have rated between –1 and –3?

Rank	Contact	−3	−2	−1	0	+1	+2	+3	Suggested improvement
1									
2									
3									
4									
5									
6									

Improving the network of contacts

Use the charts above to help you analyse whether there is anyone who should be in your network but is not yet. These can be added to the list of people with whom you need to improve communication.

Having identified the people, think about which is the most appropriate method for each of them. There are various strategies listed below but you might also find Chapters 5, 6, 35, 36 and 45 helpful.

Kotter found that the general managers created networks by:

- focusing on people they felt dependent upon or who were necessary to get things done;
- making others feel obliged to them;
- encouraging others to identify with them;
- establishing their reputation;
- making others feel dependent on them;
- replacing incompetent subordinates;
- changing suppliers and other outsiders;
- shaping the environment to encourage teamwork through structures, systems and processes.

Your Management Action

Exercises

1. The centre pages of this chapter are organized as an exercise. There are various ways of using it. You can use it to analyse your network at work. Alternatives would be to consider your last job and compare it with your present one; think about the people you know socially and the access they give you to a variety of different activities and ideas; or, if you are not currently in employment, what contacts do you have formally through your last employment, school or college, and informally that might help in finding employment?

2. List those people you talk to in the next week at work. Was the outcome satisfactory or not? Why?

3. What useful purpose do business lunches serve?

4. Is social skills training appropriate for managers or does it just reinforce a feeling of cultural superiority?

Further reading

Ferguson, M. *Aquarian Conspiracy*, J.P. Tarcher, Los Angeles, Calif., 1980.
Kotter, J.P. *The General Managers*, The Free Press, New York, 1982.

And finally . . .

Ferguson (above) notes that networking is done by

> *conferences, phone calls, air travel, books, phantom organizations, papers, pamphleteering, photocopying, lectures, workshops, parties, grapevines, mutual friends, summit meetings, coalitions, tapes, newsletters.*

17 Communication in the organization

The problems of communication in the organization are so extensive and so difficult that they can be regarded as one of management's major challenges. It is the flow of information through the organization structure, both formal and informal, that can produce understanding and action or mistrust and inefficiency. As the information flows it produces a reaction and affects working relationships and individual performance, so that the information is used to exchange ideas, attitudes and feelings.

The purposes of communication in the organization are first *general information*, which keeps members of the organization advised of matters of general interest that will affect their interest in the organization and the degree of their commitment to its affairs: progress reports, news about fresh initiatives, orders won, people appointed and so forth. *Hard information* is more specific as it is required by individuals from others to shape their own activities. The designer needs a great deal of hard information from the marketplace and from the production department to ensure that detailed design work meets the demands and difficulties of both areas. Authorization is what members of the organization seek in order to trigger a part of the administrative process, ranging from permission to engage a new employee to the acceptance of a departmental budget, or taking a day's leave for a funeral.

All of these will be influenced in their style and effectiveness by the organizational culture, so that a culture which encourages openness and trust is likely to produce plenty of general information and a ready compliance with instructions, but the main factor for us to consider here is structure and methods. If the structure of the organization puts groups in competition with each other, it will also impair the quality of communication between those groups; if it makes them mutually dependent, it will improve the quality of inter-group communication. Which is more appropriate in the situation, the cohesion and concern for task accomplishment within the groups that will be engendered by rivalry, or the collaboration and free flow of communication that will come from their mutual dependency?

The formal communications structure is represented in the pattern of working relationships and reporting, the procedures and administrative drills, the minutes of committees, the forms, the books of rules and the works of reference. The informal communications structure is to some extent the flesh on the bones of formality; it is the telephone conversations, the chats over coffee, encounters in the corridors and the confidential briefings. Although not usually 'official' these exchanges are effective at turning information into understanding and increase the number of outlets through which information passes.

Communications media

1. *The organization chart* specifies working relationships and thus identifies sources of authorization and instruction, as well as sources of hard information. Does your chart include names, telephone numbers and office locations to aid communication?

2. *Procedures and drills* show people how things should be done and specify what information is required by whom and for what purpose. Does your organization culture encourage the use or the avoidance of procedures?

3. *Reports and statements* are standardized ways of supplying factual information to a large number of people, like the monthly statement of personal earnings, deductions and cumulative pay, or the monthly performance indicators or the annual report to shareholders.

4. *Written messages* are a different form of communication as they are usually complementary to some interpersonal communication, so that their purpose is to prepare for the interpersonal exchange or to confirm its outcome: a draft report, the agenda for a meeting, the letter of invitation to an employment interview and the training manual are examples. Written messages are seldom sufficient to bring about a change in behaviour by the recipient. Do you ever rely on a written message for action only to find that the action is not taken?

5. *Electronic mail* is a way of speeding up the transmission of many written messages and reducing the number that are stored after receipt.

6. *Word of mouth* means people speaking to each other, which remains the preferred mode of communication for most matters by most people. This is not just for informal communication, but also for many formal aspects, like briefing groups, negotiations, job instruction and discipline. It is a method that provides the maximum opportunity for feedback, which is an essential ingredient of all communication. The telephone can be a fair substitute, as feedback is possible, but electronic mail is a very poor substitute for face-to-face exchange.

Communications and status

Those carrying high status in situations are encouraged to be cautious and bland in their comments about matters of high uncertainty. Their listeners will not allow them to speculate, as the need for certainty will cause them to interpret speculation as commitment. The person with little status in the organization can say 'I think we will have to close down' and then engage in discussion. The person with high status could not make that statement without it being interpreted as 'We *are* going to close down'. High status can impede and distort the feedback you receive. It can also turn casual thoughts into policy commitments.

The team briefing approach

Briefing groups are a way of using the formal organization structure to ensure regular face-to-face discussion between managers and their subordinates about matters of importance to the subordinates in their contribution to organizational success. The manager always briefs teams of subordinates rather than individuals so that a team sense is developed and contributions to the discussion will be informative to all because of the range of the interests and perspectives present. The 'cascade' principle is that the person at the top of the hierarchy briefs immediate subordinates, who then hold separate briefings of their own subordinates, and so on.

1. People are briefed collectively to enrich the information exchange.
2. The cascade idea involves a development of the briefing so that the opening message or issue is reinterpreted to be relevant to the needs of the listeners.
3. Meetings are regular (usually at fortnightly or quarterly intervals) and with a regular agenda, like the examination of a series of performance indicators.
4. Although the meetings are for two-way communication, and the briefing manager will listen and respond as well as conveying information, their purpose is briefing, not general discussion, dodging issues or airing grievances.

Some problems of organizational communication

1. *Hierarchical levels* can distort messages that are relayed through too many intermediaries. Remember how the message 'Send reinforcements, we're going to advance' became 'Send three and fourpence, we're going to a dance.'
2. *Selective perception* is the problem of our expectations leading us to hear what we expect or want to hear rather than what is intended.
3. *The credibility* of the message sender will influence the belief of the recipients in the message they receive and the action they take as a result.
4. *Information overload* is a problem mainly of written communication. Few people have the time or inclination to read long messages thoroughly and will either look for a summary (like newspaper headlines) or ask someone else to give them the gist of what the message contains.

Your Management Action

Exercises

1. For which of the following would you use only formal methods, only informal, or a combination of both formal and informal communication:

    (a) Advising employees of the date of closing down for Christmas;
    (b) A change in the annual holiday entitlement;
    (c) Proposals for a merger with another company;
    (d) A new procedure for claiming travel expenses;
    (e) Changed safety regulations.

2. An American study of the accuracy of messages being transmitted from the top to the bottom of the hierarchy in 100 companies, found that vice presidents understood 67 per cent of what they heard from directors, but the percentage then declined from 56 per cent by plant managers, 30 per cent by supervisors and 20 per cent on the shop floor. How could team briefing improve this accuracy?

Further reading

Incomes Data Services, *Employee Communications*, Study 318, IDS, London, 1984.

Thomson. F. 'The Seven Deadly Sins of Briefing Groups,' *Personnel Management*, February, 1983, pp. 32-5.

Townley, B. 'Employee Communication Programmes', in Sisson, K. (ed) *Personnel Management in Britain*, Blackwell, Oxford, 1989.

And finally . . .

*   *In 1799 Napoleon Bonaparte was leading his troops in the Middle East. 1200 Turks had been captured at Jaffa and Napoleon, it is said, was asked what should be done with them. Seized with a sudden fit of coughing, he said 'Ma sacre toux!' (My damned cough). His chief of staff understood him to say 'Massacrez tous!' (Massacre them all) and ordered the immediate execution of the 1200.*

*   *At the battle of Balaclava in 1854 the British Commander sent the order to his cavalry:*

    > *Advance and take advantage of any opportunity to recover the heights. You will be supported by infantry which have been ordered to advance on two fronts.*

    In transmission the order was distorted so that the last sentence read:

    > *You will be supported by infantry which have been ordered. Advance on two fronts.*

    The result was the infamous, futile Charge of the Light Brigade.

18   Group-working

There are several reasons why we need to have groups at work. Some tasks are performed better, or can be done only by groups of people working together. With increasing complexity of the demands on organizations no one person has all the information so groups are necessary to bring together all the required expertise to get things done. Belonging to a group can stimulate each person to greater or better effort and tends to increase job satisfaction and morale. Also, people will support that which they have helped to create, so participation in group decision-making can have useful consequences for the implementation of decisions. Working in a group provides the social satisfaction we all seek by forming informal groups.

In all human interaction there are two elements: *content* and *process*. The first deals with the subject matter or task of the interaction. The second describes how the interaction is done, how things are communicated, by whom and when. It includes the answers to such questions as: 'Who participates?', 'How do they influence others?', 'What norms of behaviour are there in the group?', and 'How are decisions arrived at?' Most of us concentrate on the content of group workings but attention to the process is extremely valuable as it is often process problems that lead to ineffective group working. This chapter is concerned with the process side of group working. The final test of an effective group is how well the task is carried out.

Bales *(1950)* developed a series of observation categories (see below) for studying the process of interaction in small groups. He found that teams needed members who kept things moving towards the goal in a co-ordinated way, and other members to ensure that relationships remained sufficiently harmonious for individuals to continue contributing to the group or team. This model has been developed by Belbin *(1981)*, who concluded that there were eight roles needed in effective management teams apart from specialist and functional roles (see below).

The process of becoming an effective group takes time, and Tuckman *(1965;* see the following page) has described the stages groups go through to increase cohesion and performance. The length of time taken for this process will vary in direct proportion to the time the group is expected to work together. If it is a permanent group, the investment is higher so everybody needs to ensure their position in the group more clearly than in a temporary group. Thus, it may take the permanent group months to go through the various stages and minutes for the one-off meeting.

Stages in the growth of group cohesion and performance

Stage of development	Process	Outcome
1. Forming	There is anxiety, dependence on leader, testing to find out the nature of the situation and what behaviour is acceptable	Members find out what the task is, what the rules are and what methods are appropriate
2. Storming	Conflict between sub-groups, rebellion against leader, opinions are polarized, resistance to control by group	Emotional resistance to demands of task
3. Norming	Development of group cohesion, norms emerge, resistance is overcome and conflicts patched up; mutual support and sense of group identity	Open exchange of views and feelings; cooperation develops
4. Performing	Interpersonal problems are resolved; interpersonal structure becomes the means of getting things done; roles are flexible and functional	Solutions to problems emerge; there are constructive attempts to complete tasks and energy is now available for effective work

Based on Tuckman (1965; pp. 384-99)

Belbin's eight roles needed in effective management teams

1. *Company worker* who keeps the organization's interests to the fore.
2. *Chairman* who ensures all views are heard and keeps things moving.
3. *Shaper* who influences by argument and by following particular topics.
4. *Ideas person* who contributes novel suggestions.
5. *Resource investigator* who evaluates whether contributions are practical and finds out where and how to get the resources.
6. *Monitor/evaluator* who assesses whether contributions are valid and to what extent the team is meeting its objectives.
7. *Team worker* who maintains the group process by joking or agreeing.
8. *Complete/finisher* who tries to get things done and suggests conclusions.

Bales's Analysis of interactions in groups

	NAMES						
SOLIDARITY							
TENSION RELEASE							
AGREES							
GIVES SUGGESTION							
GIVES OPINION							
GIVES ORIENTATION							
ASKS FOR ORIENTATION							
ASKS FOR OPINION							
ASKS FOR SUGGESTION							
DISAGREES							
SHOWS TENSION							
SHOWS ANTAGONISM							

Positive Social — SOLIDARITY, TENSION RELEASE, AGREES

Task Area — GIVES SUGGESTION, GIVES OPINION, GIVES ORIENTATION, ASKS FOR ORIENTATION, ASKS FOR OPINION, ASKS FOR SUGGESTION

Negative Social — DISAGREES, SHOWS TENSION, SHOWS ANTAGONISM

1. Put the names of team members across the top.

2. When you observe any member demonstrating any of the behaviours on the left put a stroke 1 in the appropriate box.

3. At the end of the period, meeting or week, analyse which role each member plays most frequently and which roles are not met.

4. The same sort of observation form could be used with Belbin's managerial roles.

Your Management Action

Exercises

1. Think of a group you have worked with that you enjoyed belonging to. List five reasons why this was so. Now think of a group you found frustrating to work with. List five reasons why.

2. When you are next in a meeting or group that has recently formed, try to find two examples of behaviour that indicate which stage the group has reached: forming, storming, norming or performing.

3. Use the form on the previous page in your next meeting.

4. In your next meeting, adopt a behaviour pattern that you do not normally use, either by talking a lot or not at all, or by adopting one of the behaviours in Bales's list. What was the effect?

5. Is there any difference between a committee and a team?

6. Will some of Bales's behaviours be more useful in the forming and storming phases than in the norming and performing phases of a group's working? If so, which?

7. Think of two groups you belong to. Do you play the same role in each?

8. Which of Belbin's eight management roles do you play? What about your boss? Who is the team worker and how is he or she treated?

Further reading

Bales, R.F. *Interaction Process Analysis,* Addison Wesley, London, 1950.

Belbin, R.M. *Management Teams,* Heinemann, London, 1981.

Belbin, R.M., Aston, B.R. and Mottram, R.D. Building Effective Management Teams, *Journal of General Management,* 2, 1976, pp. 23-9.

Handy, C. *Understanding Organisations,* 2nd edn, Penguin, Harmondsworth, 1981.

Schein, E.H. *Organisation Psychology,* Prentice-Hall, London, 1965.

Stewart A. and V. *Tomorrow's Managers Today,* 2nd edn, IPM, London, 1981.

Tuckman, B.W. 'Development Sequences in Small Groups', *Psychological Bulletin,* 63, 1965, 384-99.

And finally . . .

Groups fit well with a democratic culture, with representative systems of government. Participation and involvement go well with assumptions of man as an independent individual . . . But let us not be mesmerised. Let us realise that a proper understanding of groups will demonstrate how difficult they are to manage.

(Handy, 1981 p. 173)

19   Meetings

Meetings do not constitute management but are an inescapable part of the management process and are frequently less successful than they should be. It is not sufficient just to know why a meeting is being held for it to be a success: the processes by which a meeting works have to be understood as well. Poor meetings not only fail to achieve objectives; they also do harm, as members become frustrated about lack of progress or about not being able to get their point of view across. It is not just the fault of the person in charge: all participants have to learn meeting mechanics. The analogy of the orchestra is apt. The conductor is responsible for the final quality of the coordinated act, but every instrumentalist has to make a distinctive – but not individualistic – contribution that blends with all the others.

It is necessary to pay careful attention to the details of running the meeting. Good intentions and the importance of the matter to be considered are not enough on their own. The person in charge of the meeting takes the blame for things not being right. Those who feel overlooked or outmanoeuvred are merciless with those who have overlooked them, however unintentionally.

The basic necessities are a clear format, purpose and preparation, with the leader being in control. In this situation those attending the meeting can concentrate on content rather than on *process*, the way the meeting is being conducted. People will only attend and make a success of meetings they see as useful.

Few people are accustomed to expressing a point of view in a meeting and are likely to find it inhibiting. They speak best when asked to and when speaking on something about which they are knowledgeable. Leaders of meetings get contributions by asking people to speak, picking up non-verbal cues of a desire to speak or reaction to what someone else has said. Statements of fact rather than expressions of opinion are the easiest way for people to make their first contribution. Experienced members of groups can help the less experienced by 'shaping' the clumsy or over-emotional comments of their colleagues and agreeing with them (for example: 'I would like to agree with what Hilary was saying and make the further point . . .', not 'I think Hilary was trying to say . . .').

Inexperienced leaders of meetings sometimes show their worry about losing control by constantly emphasizing the limited time available, but this makes it harder for people to make coherent contributions. People speak more effectively and come to the point more quickly when not under time pressure.

The check-list

The following check-list can be used either in making the arrangements for a regular meeting, or for planning a particular meeting session.

1. **Who should attend the meeting?**
   - A large group to represent wide interests.
   - A small group to make discussion easier and more productive.
   - Representatives of each layer in the hierarchy.
   - A variety of personalities to ensure a lively discussion.
   - Only those with expertise in this area.

2. **What is the brief or terms of reference of the meeting?**
   - Does this meeting have the power to take a decision?
   - Can this meeting make a recommendation?
   - How wide can the discussion usefully range?
   - Has a decision relating to this topic already been made that cannot be changed?
   - Are there some conclusions that would be unacceptable? To whom?

3. **What should the agenda be?**
   - What do we need to consider, and in what order?
   - Is there too much to cope with?
   - Who can include items on the agenda?
   - Will matters arising and any other business take up a lot of time?

4. **What about the physical location and arrangements?**
    - Does everyone know which room and is it the right size?
    - Is the furniture arranged so that everyone can see everyone else and give them eye contact?
    - Is it appropriate to have coffee served? Has it been arranged?
    - Is it noisy, hot, cold, likely to have interruptions?

5. **How can contributions be stimulated and controlled?**
    - Who has something to say?
    - How can I get them to say it?
    - How can I keep the long-winded brief?
    - When should I nudge the meeting towards a decision/the next item?

6. **Minutes or report of the meeting**
    - Who writes these?
    - Is it important to describe the discussion and issues, or just to list the action points and who is responsible?
    - Who gets a copy of the report?
    - What will be the effect of the minutes or the report on those people who attended/did not attend?
    - Who are we trying to influence with these minutes, and in what way?

7. **Implementation of proposals**
    - Who has agreed to do what?
    - How can we help each other to get on with it?
    - Who else can we involve?
    - How can we monitor the implementation?
    - Do we need a review date?
    - What can I do to get things moving?

Your Management Action

Exercises

1. Consider a recent meeting you attended. Identify which of the following impediments to constructive discussion and subsequent action were present:

   - one or two people talking too much, some making no contribution,
   - poor agenda, no agenda,
   - poor chairing.

   What caused these impediments? Try to get through to the real reasons. For example, did the people who talked too much do so because they thought it was expected of them, because they always talk too much, because they did not understand what was happening, or for some other reason?

   How could the problems have been overcome?

2. Review another meeting you recently attended and produce two short lists:

   List A: Five lessons you have learned.

   List B: Three things you will do differently about meetings in the future.

Further reading

Belbin, R.M. *Management Teams: Why They Succeed or Fail,* Heinemann, London, 1981.

Jay, A. *Corporation Man,* Cape, London, 1972.

And finally . . .

The next time you convene a meeting, ask two questions:

1. *Is the meeting really necessary or could we use our time better?*
2. *Is a meeting the best way of achieving the declared objectives?*

20 Committees

Committees are a specialized form of group working. They have relatively formal meetings to deal with matters that are too complex, too demanding or too risky for an individual to handle alone. They also provide a way of consulting with others. Blau and Scott (1973) list the main reasons why committees are used:

1. The sifting of suggestions in social interaction helps to correct errors.
2. Thinking is helped by the social support that comes from interaction.
3. Competition among members for respect mobilizes their energies for contribution to the task.

Committee members both compete and cooperate. Although sharing the common purpose is the aim of the committee itself, they have differing personal interests and aspirations, often competing for a share of limited resources that the committee has at its disposal.

Committee members cooperate both in factions and as a whole. A faction is an alliance between some individuals to improve their competitive edge, e.g. 'Will you support me on this, if I support you on that?' The committee will operate as a whole when competition is resolved eventually by a consensus in which individual objections or reservations are withdrawn in favour of a cooperative strategy after the competing views have been aired.

The method of committee discussion is to exchange information and then to work on hypotheses. On each agenda item members first seek out the facts, even if those facts do not necessarily support their personal cause. The discussion then moves to consider alternative hypotheses, which are developed by both endorsement and critical analysis. The chairperson will look for the most acceptable in order to single it out for consent.

The main problem of committees is that they take more time than most people willingly give, and the quality of decisions may be poor. Five people meeting for two hours take 10 working hours to reach a decision, which one person might have done better working alone for five hours – or five minutes. However, this type of reservation ignores the importance of decision implementation. Five people after the meeting are committed to make work a decision that they understand already; the solo decision maker has to win commitment by time-consuming explanation. Uncertainty about the quality of decisions is based on an assumption that the need for committee members to compromise will lead to decisions that are safe rather than adventurous. This, however, has not been proven by research.

The best size of committee will depend on its main purpose. Too few can lead to insufficient input of information and ideas; too many leads to unwieldly discussion, diverse information input and inhibiting of the less confident members. Large committees are preferred where the main purpose is to brief the members or where widely differing talents and experience are needed to make decisions. Small committees are preferred where speedy decision on complex matters is needed, or where the matter under discussion is to be kept confidential.

Guidance notes for committee chairman	Guidance notes for committee member
Before the meeting	*Before the meeting*
1. What is the meeting for – decision-making, briefing, generating ideas, or something else?	1. What is the meeting for? (see 1 left)
2. Review papers for the meeting to consider timing and pacing	2. What is your role – sage, brake, synthesizer, diplomat, delegate, adviser, stimulus, or something else?
3. Review meeting arrangements with secretary	3. Review papers for meeting and notes you plan to use
During the meeting	4. Check that you have taken the action agreed for you at last meeting
4. Introduce new members	*During the meeting*
5. Call for apologies and minutes of last meeting	5. Use social skills to persuade others
6. Introduce agenda items	6. Be objective in seeking solutions that will be acceptable to others
7. Call on members to speak, seeking a balance of views, style and authority	7. Avoid personal attacks on others that would isolate you from other members
8. Focus discussion on disagreements that must be resolved	8. Support and develop contributions by others that you regard as constructive and potentially acceptable after modification
9. Periodically summarize discussion and point a new direction	9. Constantly monitor the mood of the meeting to judge when best to make your contributions – facts, opinions, suggestions or hypotheses
10. Ask for clarification from a member whose comments others find puzzling or unacceptable	10. Always 'work through the chair', recognizing the authority that the group always invests in that role
11. Pick a workable hypothesis from the discussion and choose the right time to put it to the meeting for acceptance	*After the meeting*
12. Finish on time	11. Consult with those you represent to advise them of committee decisions and required action
After the meeting	12. Study the minutes, when circulated, noting corrections needed and consider suggestions for future agenda items
13. Check with secretary that the notes or minutes of the meeting are drafted, agreed with you, and circulated	13. Take action on those items requiring your action
14. Ensure that those who have to take action know what to do, and do it	14. Review your participation; what will you do differently next time?
15. Review your role as chairman; what will you do differently next time?	

Guidance notes for committee secretary

(These notes assume that the committee meets monthly on Day 28)

Day

Minutes and preliminaries

1,2 Draft minutes, including notes of action items

5   Clear minutes with chairman and confirm date of next meeting

6,7 Type, copy and distribute minutes

7   Book room for next meeting

Agenda

12 Ask committee members for items to be included on next agenda

16 Discuss agenda items and sequence with chairman
    Suggested sequence:
    (a) Introduction of new members; apologies for absence
    (b) Minutes of previous meeting reviewed for accuracy
    (c) Matters arising from minutes and not appearing on agenda
    (d) Items for decision and causing little controversy
    (e) Most difficult item
    (f) Next most difficult item
    (g) Items requiring discussion but not decision
    (h) Easy items
    (i) Any other business
    (j) Provisional date for next meeting

Run-up

19 Circulate agenda and other papers

23 Check room arrangements

27 Collate all papers, past minutes, apologies

The meeting

28 (a) Supply papers to chairman in agenda sequence
    (b) Take general notes of discussion in order to provide information, if needed, on earlier points as meeting proceeds
    (c) Take precise notes of matters agreed and of who is to take action
    (d) Remain detached from discussion except for providing information or seeking clarification

The main art of *chairing* a committee is in maintaining a balance between the stimulus of competition and a reasonably secure, agreeable atmosphere for discussion. Competition between members must not reach a point where it destroys the possibility of cooperation and making progress.	The best *committee members* are essential to the purpose and not people who might be useful. They should be interested in its purpose, with some stake in its success, and should have relevant knowledge and experience. They should have enough time to attend and prepare for meetings.

Your Management Action

Exercises

1. The next time you attend a committee meeting, see if your fellow committee members can be categorized in the way suggested by our guidance notes on the previous page: sage, brake, synthesizer, diplomat, delegate, adviser, stimulus. Is there an important role missing? Is there a good balance, or are too many people filling one or two roles? Does the committee need a change of membership?

2. At a meeting concentrate your own mode of participation in the form suggested in the guidance notes on the previous page (4 – 12 for chairman, 5 – 10 for members). What effect did your change of mode have?

3. President J.F. Kennedy is alleged to have said about committees: 'Everyone is the father of success; failure is an orphan.' Think through the committees which you attend and identify the ways in which the number of orphans can be reduced.

Further reading

Blau, P.M. and Scott, W.R. 'Processes of Communication in Formal Organizations', in Argyle, M. (ed.) *Social Encounters*, Penguin, Harmondsworth, 1973.

Schwartz, D.F. *Introduction to Management: Principles, Practices and Processes*, Harcourt, Brace, Jovanovich, New York, 1980.

Smith, P.B. *Groups within Organizations*, Harper and Row, London, 1973.

Summers, I. and White, D.E. 'Creativity Techniques: Towards Improvements in the Decision Process', *The Academy of Management Review*, April, 1976, pp. 14-22.

And finally . . .

There are three main forms of committee:

1. *The* plural *executive is a decision-making body of people who all carry a share of responsibility individually and who can make a collective decision through all having a stake in the matters being discussed.*

2. *The* linking pin *is a group with the purpose of keeping people in a complex organization informed about what is happening. Members with varied responsibilities come to brief others, to be briefed, and to take away messages for others.*

3. *The* think tank *is a group of people who serve an advisory purpose by working out strategies and rough-cut decisions for others to accept, reject or modify before taking action.*

21 Dealing with change

Change has become so much a part of our expectations both at work and in our private lives that we need to develop strategies to deal with it. Most of us are unsettled by uncertainty and try to control, predict and maintain things in their present state as this is more comfortable. Toffler (1970) argues that we are dazzled by change which we cannot understand and he maintains we need to have stability zones (see Chapter 11 of this book) so we can deal with the change happening around us. In his later book Toffler (1980) argues that we are now less terrified of change and are beginning to deal more successfully with it.

Managers not only need to deal with change at the personal level but also need to influence what changes are to happen and occasionally to initiate change. These changes may be required for a variety of reasons: competitive position, reducing expenditure, more efficient, easier, pleasanter, change in personnel, change in available resources, political pressure, outside influences, internal reasons or purely personal factors. Having analysed why a change is necessary managers need to decide what alterations to make and how to implement them. Changes can be anything from major reorganizations where most members have their work altered or removed, to small changes in procedure. All changes need careful consideration to ensure that the desired effect has the maximum chance of happening.

Managers not only need to influence what changes are to happen but frequently have to deal with change imposed from elsewhere. This is when the reasons for change, what changes and how are all decided elsewhere. Managers, usually middle or junior, are left with the job of implementing change they have not taken part in deciding and may not agree with. Getting subordinates, who in turn have not been involved in the decision-taking nor necessarily agree with the changes, to comply, is one of the more difficult and challenging tasks of management. Particularly where the change is one of rationalization, reduction and retrenchment after a period of uncertainty.

Dealing with change also has a political aspect. Those who can deal with uncertainty and find the solution are the more powerful. Where this also involves some prediction of how the future might be, power is even greater. This power becomes authority by being legitimized through increased status being given to those who forecast and plan for change. Some may have expertise in the area and so become authorities; others are those with job titles higher up the hierarchy and in authority. There is an interaction whereby those with authority claim the right to determine what changes are made and those who deal with change become authorities. Consequently, it is important for managers to deal with change because it is intrinsically linked with their role as managers.

Managers have two choices: they can let change happen to them with all the anxiety of uncertainty, or they can deal with change and influence some of the change taking place. Either way, change cannot be ignored.

Why make a change?

- Are you sure the change you are suggesting is useful? Is it just a desire to make an impact for career reasons? What objectives or outcomes will be beneficial as a result of this change?

- Do others agree that change is necessary?

- Problem-solving techniques (see Chapter 7) can be applied in analysing what change might be useful.

- Inventiveness is more likely when:
  1. *notes* are kept of moments of insight which usually come in periods of rest after working hard on the problem;
  2. *deadlines and quotas* are set which ensure people try to find solutions rather than putting off the problem till later;
  3. *time and place* are set aside for generating ideas which otherwise would get squeezed out by other demands;
  4. *listening and rewarding* innovative ideas within the department or organization.

Dissemination

- Influencing and persuading other people that the idea is fruitful is necessary to get things changed (see part B of this book). They need to be persuaded that the proposal is not only new but an improved method.

- It is necessary to get sufficient commitment that resources are made available, with a budget to evaluate the feasibility of the proposed change.

Implementing

- Change is easier to implement if people see it as being in their interest and they are involved in the change. Those who have made the decision are committed to making it work.

- There are three phases to change. Different people are better at managing each phase.
  1. *Unfreeze*   people are made ready to learn
  2. *Change*   the change or learning takes place
  3. *Refreeze*   the change is consolidated.

Participation

How one implements change will vary with the type of participation that is practised in the organization or department. In some the convention will be that there is extensive consultation to win consent for what is proposed; in others change will be implemented by decree. The figure below lists categories of consent sought in different organizations before implementing change.

Category of employee consent

1. *Controlling* When there is employee control, as in a cooperative, managers are authorized to act by the employees.

2. *Participative* Employees do not control the business, but participate in decision-making on major issues.

3. *Negotiated* Employees limit the freedom of managers to introduce change through the separation of some matters on which action can be based only on some form of mutual accommodation.

4. *Consultative* Managers ask for the opinions of employees before implementing change, although the opinions may be partly or completely ignored.

5. *Grudging* Where managers are not willing to consult on decisions, or where unions are not strong enough to require consultation, there will be no explicit challenge from employees, but this does not necessarily mean commitment.

6. *Normative* In some organizations there is a strong sense of moral obligation to the leadership which is engendered among the employees. Any challenge or questioning would be unthinkable as it would imply a refutation of the shared values, or norms.

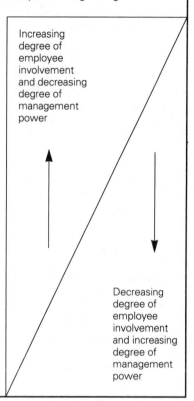

Increasing degree of employee involvement and decreasing degree of management power

Decreasing degree of employee involvement and increasing degree of management power

Consequences

All changes have consequences that are unintended as well as intended. Some of these are beneficial; others are not. Managers like to reduce to the minimum the unintended consequences of their change initiatives. It is worth spending time brainstorming (see Chapter 41) to think of all the possible consequences of a proposed course of action.

Your Management Action

Exercises

1. Next time an idea is put to you, first list the reasons for rejecting it and then list the reasons for supporting it.

2. What types of uncertainty do other people present to you for resolution? Is this on the basis of expertise or position?

3. Try keeping a piece of paper with you at all times for the next week and whenever a potentially constructive thought comes to you write it down without evaluating it in any way. At the end of the week look through the list and see if there are any interesting ideas.

4. Who would you have to influence and persuade first if you wanted to change what you do at work?

5. In a period of change are you someone whose first instinct is to question the sense of the change or are you someone who enjoys constant change?

6. What sort of participation does your boss practise and what sort do you practise? One question to test this is to ask: 'What are the consequences when those lower in the hierarchy disagree?'

Further reading

Drucker, P.F. *The New Realities*, Mandarin, London, 1990.
Taylor, D.E. and Singer, E.J. *New Organizations from Old*, Institute of Personnel Management, London, 1983.
Toffler, A. *Future Shock*, Random House, New York, 1970.
Toffler, A. *The Third Wave*, Morrow, New York, 1980.

And finally . . .

No one knows in detail what the future holds or what will work best . . . For this reason we should think not of a single massive reorganization nor of a single revolutionary, cataclysmic change imposed from the top, but of thousands of conscious, decentralized experiments . . .

                                                        (Toffler, 1980, p. 452.)

22 Policy and strategy

Strategy is about what you are trying to achieve and where you are trying to go. Policy provides a framework within which strategy and all the other activities of the business will be conducted.

Stoner and Wanel *(1986)* provide contrasted definitions:

> [Strategy is] the broad program for defining and achieving an organization's objectives; the organization's response to its environment over time. (p. 695)

> A policy is a general guideline for decision-making. It sets up boundaries around decisions, including those that can be made and shutting out those that cannot. In this way it channels the thinking of organization members so that it is consistent with organizational objectives. Some policies deal with very important matters, like those requiring strict sanitary conditions where food or drugs are produced or packaged. Others may be concerned with relatively minor issues, such as the way the employees dress. (p. 91)

An example will illustrate the difference. To meet expansion requirements a company has decided to open a new sales and service centre in Bradford and they want to start trading from the new centre without their competitors knowing in advance. This main *strategy* is then developed with further decisions on the number of people needed for the new operation, with what skills and with what facilities. A further set of decisions concern the type of premises and the range of services within the premises. Then it is decided how to set about locating and employing the necessary people, the sequence in which they are to be engaged and the employment costs of each category, all of which constitutes strategy.

Alongside, there will be *policy* decisions on whether or not vacancies in the new centre will be made known to existing employees, what methods of recruitment and selection will be used, what type of remuneration package will be offered and how legal obligations in matters such as health and safety and employment rights are to be met. This is the policy to frame the strategy.

Strategy is nearly always new and changing to take advantage of fresh opportunities. Policy has less novelty as there is a continuously evolving framework, even though each new activity tends to throw up considerations that have not occurred previously.

There is *always* a policy. If the management have not devised one, then the policy in practice is what has happened before, that is precedents.

Why all the fuss about strategy?

Strategy has been of great importance in the late 1980s because of its emphasis on creating the future rather than waiting for it to come round the corner and punch you on the nose; or waiting for a future that *never does* come round the corner. Strategic thinking provides a clear sense of direction and focus on where the business is going. Although obvious, this simple clarification and possible change in emphasis can have a profound effect. If, for instance, you are running an airport, what business are you in – providing parking space for aeroplanes, providing a service for airlines, providing an agreeable, efficient service for passengers, or something else? From a clear sense of purpose specific objectives can be derived.

Concern with strategy can go too far: it can become the dominant activity of managers rather than a means whereby they run the business. Thought is no substitute for action, plans are not an alternative to operations and analysis can aid but never replace judgement. There is the possibility of becoming so rational in decision-making that only safe courses of action are pursued and opportunities are lost or elementary errors are made.

There is also the risk that the association of strategy with top people, causes a rush of blood to the heads of those who aspire to greatness without actually having it. Everyone in a business needs to think strategically, but thinking strategically does not exonerate you from doing the work.

The characteristics of strategic decisions

Strategic decisions are concerned with:

- The scope of an organization's activities.
- The matching of an organization's activities to its environment.
- The matching of the activities of an organization to its resource capability.
- The allocation and reallocation of major resources in an organization.
- The values, expectations and goals of those influencing strategy.
- The direction an organization will move in the long term.
- Implications for change throughout the organization – they are therefore likely to be complex in nature.

(Johnson and Scholes, 1989, p. 8.)

Six reasons for having policies

Policies can be a problem. If your policy does not work, you are incompetent; if your policy is unpopular, your enemies try to undermine it; if your policy is accepted, you will have little chance of changing it. Why bother? Why not treat each case on its merits? Here are some reasons.

1. *Policy can change things* In all areas there is a tendency for things to be done the way they always have been done and any individual manager will find this dependence on precedent hard to fight. Getting agreement to a new policy is the best way of breaking with the past.

2. *Policy can clarify a manager's position* Managers regularly seek endorsement of their strategies from colleagues, by getting their budgets approved or their plans accepted. In making this type of bid a statement of policy on how, as well as for what, the money is to be used increases the strength of the case.

3. *Policy can make the management's position clear* People at work increasingly expect to be supplied with information and guidance about management intentions for the future.

4. *Policy makes managers behave in a consistent way* Policy provides a useful discipline for managers as they have to behave in a consistent way. Some managers resist the need to behave consistently, feeling that it blunts their creative drive, but they soon find that a policy framework prevents them from wasting time and energy working out new solutions to problems that have already been solved, and enables them to concentrate on where initiative and imagination are really needed.

5. *Policy shapes the response to imposed change* Frequently organizations are faced with changes being dumped on them from outside, and managers then await policy guidance so that they know what to do. When a new piece of legislation is introduced managers will receive information about what the legislation intends, but they will await an organizational initiative before taking any action. 'How are *we* going to respond to this change?' If there is no policy guidance, there will be no management initiative until a crisis occurs.

6. *Policy can reduce dependence on individuals* If there is a policy to follow, then there is less need always 'to consult the oracle' to find out what to do: you can look it up instead. Splendid individuals are no substitute for sound policies.

A three-part rule for policy formulation

1. Policy does not produce effective practice without commitment to both the policy and measures to make it work.

2. Commitment is more likely when the policy is developed from issues in the organization itself.

3. The policy is devised, and later sustained, by the involvement of all those affected by it.

Your Management Action

Exercises

1. Obtain a policy document from your organization, for instance on health and safety or equal opportunity, and review it against these questions:
   - What is its purpose and how well does it succeed?
   - How would you improve it?
   - Are your improvements feasible?
   - Why were they necessary?
   - How could they be implemented?
   - What strategic action are you now going to take?

2. Devise a policy to determine allocation of annual leave dates for you and your colleagues.
   - What would be your guiding principles?
   - With whom would you consult?
   - How would you publicize the result?

Further reading

Georgiades, N. 'A Strategic Future for Personnel?', *Personnel Management*, February, 1990.

Johnson, B. and Scholes, K. *Exploring Corporate Strategy*, Prentice-Hall, Hemel Hempstead, 1989.

Stoner, J.A.F. and Wankel, C. *Management*, 3rd edn, Prentice-Hall, Englewood Cliffs, New Jersey, 1986.

And finally . . .

A comment from a stock allocator in a retail chain:

> *Policy is just an excuse for a jack-in-office to tell me what I cannot do and to slow down the implementation of what I have to do. My section is expanding fast and we have agreement for the recruitment of two new girls. We have the budget, we are hellishly busy, but we cannot recruit yet because of 'policy'. I have had to send explanatory memos to three different people at head office, my draft advertisements have been sent back for revision because I used the word 'her' once. I know that was a mistake, but as a woman I get really pissed off when one middle-aged male ticks me off in a sarky way for breaching the equal opportunity policy. We want to get on and do things. Policy just holds you back.*

Part C

Managing to get things done

23 Procedures for administrative action

Procedures get things done. Splendid ideas and bold decisions will be of little value without precise and efficient procedures to translate intention into action.

There are four main benefits of procedures.

1. They reduce the need for decisions in the future. When the solution to a problem has been worked out once, the procedure provides a model for dealing with the same problem when it recurs. The procedure is a recipe, and the necessary action can be taken more quickly and by more people in an identical way than if it had to be worked out afresh.

2. Procedures produce consistency of action. If things are always done in the same way, those who are involved become practised in their dealings. Retail outlets develop similar procedures for dealing with customers, so that a customer will frequently need to ask only one question: 'Do you serve yourself or does someone serve you?' before being able to move smoothly through the purchasing routine. Employees also become accustomed to procedural drills and are able to work together swiftly and harmoniously as long as methods are unaltered.

3. Procedures provide a form of control for management. Managers know that the system will keep things working correctly and smoothly, so that they can turn their attention to future challenges and current problems without being distracted by constant requests for guidance and information.

4. There is also the benefit of freedom from supervision. Learner drivers are under constant supervision during their first lesson, but as they learn the procedures of driving, supervision becomes less overbearing. The good administrative procedure gives staff members information and authority, so that they know what to do and how to do it, with scope to interpret the rules in unexpected situations. In this way, the benefits of management control are accompanied by the advantages of individual autonomy.

The biggest problem with procedures is that they are dull, so that few managers like to invest the time needed to get them right. Other problems can be that procedures inhibit change by providing a secure and familiar routine that people are reluctant to abandon. There is sometimes a problem of duplication, where one department has a procedure for its own stage in affairs which does not coincide with that of the next department in sequence. In producing a standard way of doing things, procedure may be interpreted as the only way of doing things and thus bring problems of rigidity. When procedural rigidity confronts managerial enthusiasm or employee discontent, enthusiasm undermines by 'cutting through the red tape' and discontent overcomes rigidity by 'short-circuiting the system'. The procedure will then collapse or become obsolete.

Procedures are developed by applying logic to common sense and understanding. Three common methods of finding a framework are the *check-list, modelling,* and *flow charting.*

1. Check-list of procedure principles

1. What are *all* the objectives you want to achieve?

2. Which are not really needed because there is already a satisfactory method, or because procedure is not the right answer to the problem?

3. What are the starting and finishing points of the procedure?

4. What are the interim steps to be? They should be:

    (a) as few as possible

    (b) as simple as possible

    (c) clear and logical

    (d) as complete as possible

5. Pilot the procedure by trying it out in circumstances as realistic as possible.

6. Modify procedure in the light of pilot run; re-test.

7. Implement procedure and monitor effectiveness.

2. Model of instruction procedure

1. Set behavioural objectives. Decide what the trainee will be able to do when the training is complete.

2. Choose training method.

3. Meet trainee to explain what has to be done, when various standards of attainment will be reached and what the benefits of success are, giving the trainee confidence in his or her ability to succeed.

4. Present task by showing the trainee what to do: first the complete task, and then the first stage which the trainee has to master.

5. Supervise practice as trainee practises each stage in turn until the appropriate standard is reached.

6. Reinforce growing competence of trainee by explaining when something is done well and showing how overall ability is being developed. Problems are also pointed out, but with the solution also shown.

7. Evaluate instruction after each trainee has finished to see if the method or procedure can be improved.

3. Flow charting

This method is used for detailed and complex administrative procedures where check-lists or models would not be sufficient to encompass all the variables. The standard symbols used in flow charting are:

Operation ◯	Inspection ☐
Transport ▷	Delay ▷
Storage ▽	

4. Sample of procedure flow chart: progress of a sales order form

Sales	Stock control	Trans- port	Ware- house	Finance	

Salesman takes order

Order passed to sales order clerk

7-part order form (OF) produced

Copy no. 7 filed

OF passed to stock control

Stock level checked

Warehouse location noted on OF

Copy no. 6 filed

OF passed to transport division

Driver/vehicle availability checked

Driver/vehicle allocated

Copy no. 5 filed

OF passed to warehouse

OF passed to driver

Location of goods checked

Delivery date awaited

Collection of order recorded on OF

Copy no. 4 filed

OF passed to finance department

Invoice procedures completed

Copy no. 3 filed

OF endorsed by customer as proof of delivery

Copy no. 2 left with customer

OF passed to stock control

Stock levels checked

Stock re-ordered if necessary

Copy no. 1 filed

Your Management Action

Exercises

1. Assume that one of the following policy decisions has been taken in your organization:

    (a) 10 per cent of the employees are to be made redundant;
    (b) Product advertising is to be moved from national dailies to television;
    (c) Numerically controlled machines are to be introduced for the first time;
    (d) A major new line of business is to be introduced.

    Use the check-list principles on the previous page to devise a procedure to advise all those who need to know, ensuring the correct sequence of people to be informed and the necessary degree of detailed information.

2. Use the model procedure for instruction to prepare to teach someone how to carry out a series of actions successfully, such as a recipe in cookery, a conjuring trick, or wiring a plug.

3. Think of a procedure in your organization which you know well, but which you regard as unsatisfactory, and use the flow chart method to devise an improved version.

Further reading

Carter, R. *Business Administration*, Heinemann, London, 1982.

Cyert, R.M. and March, J.G. *A Behavioural Theory of the Firm*, Prentice-Hall, Englewood Cliffs, New Jersey, 1963.

Singleton, N. *Industrial Relations Procedures*, HMSO, London, 1975.

And finally . . .

Procedures have been described as the link between policy *('what we would like to happen') and* practice *('what is happening'). Policy is a general statement of intention, like those in Exercise 1 above, which has to be communicated to members of the organization, not only for them to be advised, but also for them to be convinced that the policy is appropriate. However, the policy statements also need procedures to make them work.*

Policies that fail may be poor decisions or good decisions that people elsewhere in the organization never understood, but most often they are good decisions that foundered because there was no procedural follow-through.

Procedures are no substitute for policy decisions, and they are no answer to organizational problems requiring a policy solution.

24   Goal planning and target setting

If managers are to lead working teams, they must know where they are heading. They need to be constantly thinking ahead and deciding what goals to aim for, and the best means of reaching them. This is the activity of planning. However, planning has a poor reputation among managers because of the frequency with which plans turn out to be unworkable, and can hamper initiative because unplanned activities are not legitimate. There is also the danger of spending more time refining the predictions and less time on getting on with the job that has to be done. Some organization of ideas and arrangements for the future is nonetheless essential to the management role.

Planning is used in various ways in management. One easy distinction is how far in the future the plans are for. Hogarth and Makridakis *(1981)* give a comprehensive review of the literature on forecasting and planning. Long range or strategic forecasting and planning which looks at least two years ahead is notoriously inaccurate. This is because of difficulties in assessing the size of forecast errors, unforeseen changes in trends, discontinuities and new events and conditions. Medium-term plans, for between three months and two years, are theoretically derived from long-term plans, estimates of available resources, constraints and competitive considerations. The most common forms are operational budgets that act also as control mechanisms. Short-term planning, for three months or less, can be reasonably accurate because of the considerable inertia in most economic and natural phenomena. Hogarth and Makridakis conclude that simple models can often be as accurate and effective as sophisticated or elaborate models. Despite these reservations planning is felt by most managers to be necessary so that they are proactive: taking initiatives and making things happen, rather than being reactive: merely responding to situations as they occur.

This chapter is about short-term planning by individual managers. Goals or targets are statements of what you are trying to do and what the priorities are. Answers to these basic questions help managers deploy resources effectively and achieve neither too much nor too little. Goal planning is the process by which it is aimed to achieve the goal. It includes an assessment of the present position, how far from the goal this is, what resources are available, what will help to achieve the goal and what will hinder its achievement. Objectives are specific parts of the process that need to be met to achieve the goal. They are the detailed strategies and tasks that are the means by which the end is achieved. They are most usefully thought out in specific statements so it is clear when they are done.

Goal planning, target setting and objectives are most usefully employed when other strategies are not working. The technique is useful also where it is felt the goal will not be reached by other means, such as introducing new methods or changing old ones.

Goal planning and target setting

1. Decide what your goal or target is. Write it down with the criteria you will use to judge whether the goal has been met.

2. List the strengths you have already that will help you achieve the goal. Examples of the areas you might think about are given below.

3. List what you still need to reach your goal. Write these as concretely as possible so you can tell when you have met the need and it has become a strength. Using the same list as before might help you to think about all the areas.

4. If a need is particularly difficult to achieve use the form opposite to break the need into smaller, more easily achieved objectives.

Goal or target

Strengths	*Needs*
1. Time	
2. Place	
3. Money	
4. Materials	
5. Cooperation of . . .	
6. Agreement of . . .	
7. Expertise	
8.	
9.	
10.	

Setting objectives

1. Objectives can be to meet goals and targets set by oneself or others.

2. Make a list of the various possible ways of achieving the goal. Asking others for their ideas may increase your list of options but they are likely to be disappointed if their idea is not used (see Chapter 41 on Brainstorming for other strategies).

3. Decide which is the most appropriate method by comparing the advantages and disadvantages of each.

4. The goal-planning forms can be used to establish the strengths and needs of reaching the goal in this way.

5. When dividing the needs into specific objectives it is advisable to state them so that an answer 'yes, that is done' can be given or not. Dead-lines help the constantly interrupted manager.

Need

Objective	Method	Target date	Date done
1.			
2.			
3.			
4.			
5.			
6.			

Your Management Action

Exercises

1. Try using the goal planning forms on something you have not quite managed to do recently. This could be something personal or at work.

2. Put the following general aims into operational form, by writing down the criteria that will determine whether or not the objectives have been achieved. If, for example, the aim was 'Get agreement on budget', this might be operationalized as 'Get AB, CD and EF to agree the travel budget by 10 February'. You then have three activities to undertake, and know that completing the activities will achieve the aim:
    (a) Encourage staff to do better
    (b) Make more visits to customers
    (c) Be a better spouse
    (d) Monitor budget more often

3. Turn five of the aims you have for next week into operational form. When they are completed, put dates by them.

Further reading

Hogarth, R.M. and Makridakis, S. 'Forecasting and Planning: An Evaluation', *Management Science*, 1981, vol. 27, no. 2, pp. 72-4, reprinted in abbreviated form in Paton, R. *et al.* (eds) *Organizations: Cases, Issues, Concepts*, Harper and Row, London, 1984.

Macbrien, J.A. *Final Report of the EDY Project to the DES*, Manchester University Press, Manchester, 1981.

And finally . . .

The value of goal planning and target setting lies in getting started. Ambitious plans sometimes fail because the planners see the ultimate objective clearly in pristine glory but are not interested in the painstaking steps needed to reach that goal. With its emphasis on the short term, goal planning provides a means of getting through the maze of minor problems that stand between the planners and the achievement of their objective.

25 Job analysis

Job analysis is the process of systematically and logically examining a job in detail to identify its components. It has long been one of the basic techniques of the personnel specialist and has an extensive range of applications.

Currently the most common use is in payment, where the analysis produces a job description, which can be used to justify a pay differential between job A and job B. A second application is in recruitment and selection, where the method has been used longest. The analysis here produces a job description, so that the recruiter can then set about looking for the appropriate type of person, as well as providing summary information for the applicant. A similar application is in performance appraisal, to assist the comparison of performance with expectation. In training, analysis produces not only the job description but also the training drill or manual, so that the new recruit is taught how to perform the various components of the job. Other applications are in establishing equal value, manpower planning, departmental staffing and sorting out problems of organization, as mentioned in Chapter 12.

The standard products of job analysis are first the job description, which is a statement of the purpose, scope, responsibilities and tasks which constitute a particular job. Second is a personnel specification, which is a statement about the knowledge and skills required to meet the demands of the job description. The job description is an invariable requirement, while the personnel specification is only needed in some applications. There is always a temptation to ignore the job description and go straight to the specification: 'another Pat Smith would be ideal', but what made Pat Smith ideal was as much a feature of the job as of Pat Smith.

The most common form of job analysis is the check-list, where the answers to a series of standard questions are integrated into a job description. This can be done by the job holder, by a combination of job holder and supervisor, by the supervisor, or by a specialist job analyst. Although the job holder has the most intimate knowledge of the job, he or she may not emphasize the points most relevant for the particular application. A job analyst is an expert, but there is seldom a sufficient demand to justify such an appointment. A less popular method is the written narrative, where the job is described without the benefit or constraint of a standard format. Various forms of observation provide the most detailed analysis and the best scope for work rationalization through the techniques of work study.

There is no standard method that can be advocated, because of the range of applications. A job description to be used in selection, for instance, will emphasize job content as a means towards a personnel specification and a discriminating advertisement attracting only those likely to be successful. In payment applications, however, the emphasis is on the difference between jobs. The two applications require different approaches, as seen in the alternatives on the next two pages.

Part of a job analysis check-list for use in job evaluation

1. Job title ....

2. General statement of duties ....

3. Level of education required
   - (a) Basic secondary ☐
   - (b) 4 – 6 GCSE O levels ☐
   - (c) 2 GCE A levels ☐
   - (d) Degree in .... ☐
   - (e) Postgraduate professional qualification ☐

4. Amount of previous similar or related work experience necessary for a person starting this job
   - (a) None ☐
   - (b) Less than 3 months ☐
   - (c) 3 months to 1 year ☐
   - (d) 1 to 3 years ☐

5. How much supervision does the job require?
   - (a) Frequent ☐
   - (b) Several times daily ☐
   - (c) Occasional ☐
   - (d) Limited ☐
   - (e) Little or none ☐

6. Number of people supervised by job holder
   - (a) None ☐
   - (b) 1 ☐
   - (c) 2 – 5 ☐
   - (d) 6 – 20 ☐
   - (e) 21 – 50 ☐
   - (f) 51 + ☐

7. Cost to organization of errors made by job holder
   - (a) Under £25 ☐
   - (b) £25 – £100 ☐
   - (c) £100 – £500 ☐
   - (d) £500 – £5,000 ☐
   - (e) More than £5,000 ☐

8. How often is the possibility of such errors checked?
   - (a) Daily ☐
   - (b) Weekly ☐
   - (c) Monthly ☐
   - (d) Quarterly ☐
   - (e) Annually ☐
   - (f) Not regularly checked ☐

9. Contacts with other people initiated by job holder

	Constantly	Often	Occasionally	Never
In own department				
In other departments				
With suppliers				
With customers				
With civic authorities				
Other				

10. Aspects of the job involving confidentiality/security

....

11. Disagreeble/dangerous aspects of job

....

12. Resourcefulness or initiative required

....

Job analysis check-list to produce job description for selection

1.   Job title

2.   Duties and range of responsibility
    (a) What has to be done
    (b) Relationship of job to rest of organization
    (c) Extent of responsibility
    (d) Overall purpose of the job

3.   Relationships
    (a) Job holder reports to . . .
    (b) Reporting to job holder are . . .
    (c) Nature of these and other contacts

4.   Physical environment
    (a) Where job is done
    (b) Hours and days of work
    (c) Health or accident hazards

5.   Conditions of employment
    (a) Salary
    (b) Salary review arrangements
    (c) Pension and sick pay
    (d) Fringe benefits

6.   Future prospects

Matrix for preparing personnel specification

Job title ....

	Essential	Desirable	Dangerous
Education and qualifications			
Knowledge and skills			
Working experience			
Disposition			
Aptitudes			
Circumstances			
Attitudes			
Age			
Car driver			
Union member			

Your Management Action

Exercises

1. In your organization, for which of the applications mentioned in this chapter is job analysis used? Where could it be usefully introduced?

2. How can you produce job descriptions that are a useful framework for action without becoming straitjackets denying people scope or 'defensive guarantees' behind which people shelter to avoid additional demands?

3. What, if any, is the scope of using job descriptions for management control of operations?

Further reading

Advisory, Conciliation and Arbitration Service (ACAS). *Job Evaluation*, ACAS, London, 1984.

Torrington, D.P. and Hall, L.A. *Personnel Management: A New Approach*, 2nd edn, Prentice-Hall, Hemel Hempstead, 1991.

(In addition, all texts on personnel management have sections devoted to job analysis techniques.)

And finally . . .

A useful but novel method of detailing job descriptions is by using management teams. Each team member sets aside a weekend for the activity and writes out a personal job description, according to an agreed format. Then team members exchange copies with each other and study the complete set before a long, full meeting of all participants at which they pick up all the gaps and overlaps between them and find acceptable ways of dealing with problems.

All members have to work through the parameters of their jobs and explain aspects on which others ask for clarification. The process will not only plug gaps and make sure that responsibilities fit together constructively, it will also produce a model of working together afterwards that will probably be more effective than could be achieved by any other means, as potential gaps in responsibility between manager A and manager B have been worked on not just by those two, but by all their other colleagues as well. This results in wide-ranging understanding and appreciation.

A weekend is needed to ensure that issues are talked out thoroughly and not glossed.

26 Activity scheduling

'The first step towards understanding work', comments Drucker (1974), 'is to analyse it'. Knowledge of the 'syntax' of work activities, their relationships, connections and configuration, enables management to plan, control and evaluate the steps which are being undertaken to achieve the desired end. Techniques such as goal planning, target setting, forecasting trends and developing systems (all discussed in other chapters) are processes which help determine the nature of future activities of the organization by asking the question 'Where do we want to be?', and then 'How do we get there?'. Activity scheduling is another such technique.

Functions such as purchasing, marketing, production, personnel and finance all involve activities which have to be scheduled in order to meet commitments within constraints. Achieving a satisfactory balance between the utilization of resources and the level of service offered is the principal objective of activity scheduling.

One method which provides a basis for many schedules is that of Gantt charting, named after its originator. This is a visual display (see next two pages for examples) of the planned order of activities over a period which allows for continuous monitoring and control while the plan is in operation. Activities are listed down one side, and the time taken by each activity is represented by a horizontal line, measured in minutes, days, weeks, or months as appropriate. To show how work is progressing, a bar or line is superimposed which represents the amount of work actually completed at stated times. Gantt chart schedules may be built up forwards with each job being scheduled as early as possible after completion of a previous job, or backwards, working back from the 'due-date' in order to determine the start date for the operation. They may be used to show the schedule of work for one particular operation from start to finish, to show the work load on one piece of equipment or machinery, to monitor progress or to display work patterns and rotas for groups of people. These charts can be highly informative, combining both the planning and recording of progress where their use has been highly developed. Gantt charts can also show the interrelationships between activities, e.g. a requirement that two activities must be completed before the third activity is started.

Where there are hundreds or thousands of operations to be scheduled, it may become impossible to use manually composed schedules, since the delay of one operation may require the rearrangement of many others. In these circumstances, Gantt charts may be constructed using computer programmes, taking care that a schedule produced in this manner is realistic and is attainable rather than merely 'optimum'.

Schedules should not be kept locked away in the manager's desk. As dynamic aids to planning and control, they should be openly displayed on the office wall or workshop noticeboard and continuously updated. By using a daily update system, supervisors and staff will develop confidence in the schedules and their relationship to their actual work.

Activity scheduling – aims, preparation, problems, effectiveness

Examples of some aims and objectives of scheduling
Completion of work by due date; maximization of output, minimization of operator/machine idle time; minimization of material waiting time, minimization of costs, maintenance of even balance of work load and work flow; maintenance of balance of equipment utilization and labour utilization, provision of information on which to base realisitic and reliable delivery promises.

Possible factors to consider in the preparation of schedules
Existing commitments; available resources; machine and operator efficiency; work content of task under consideration; method and sequence of task components; maintenance commitments; holidays and training; allowances for sickness, absenteeism, reject work, machine breakdown (facilities may be loaded to 75 per cent, for example, to allow for potential delay).

Potential problems in scheduling
- Failure to identify objectives; large variety of component tasks and methods; material shortages; accuracy of data; changes to schedule.
- Failure of top management to understand the importance and implication of planning and control through scheduling. This results in the absence of defined responsibilities; formation of unambiguous company policy; appropriate training and recruitment activities, non-preferential delivery promises.
- Failure of line management to adhere to the schedules; establish feedback mechanisms for job progress; devise systems for updating schedules and revising priorities at frequent intervals; distribute information to operating personnel.

Some measures of effective scheduling
Level of output; percentage resource utilization; number of clients/customers; client/customer; 'queueing' time; percentage orders delivered on or before due-date; percentage shortages or stock-outs; number of complaints.

With acknowledgements to B. Dale

A   An example of a shift rota

Team	January															
	1	2	3	4	5	6	7	8	9	10	11	12	13	14	15	16 etc
A	D	D	N	N	–	–	–	–	D	D	N	N	–	–	–	–
B	–	–	D	D	N	N	–	–	–	–	D	D	N	N	–	–
C	–	–	–	–	D	D	N	N	–	–	–	–	D	D	N	N
D	N	N	–	–	–	–	D	D	N	N	–	–	–	–	D	D

Four-shift system: each team works two 12-hour day shifts, two 12-hour night shifts, then has four days off.

B   An example of a Sales Progress chart

Sales Programme: units sold as at week 22

		April				May				June			
Week no.	14	15	16	17	18	19	20	21	22	23	24	25	26
Product A	80	80	60	80	80	80	80	80	80	80	80	80	80
Product B	–	–	–	–	–	40	60	60	60	60	60	60	70
Product C	40	40	40	40	40	40	40	40	40	40	40	40	40

The lines show progress up to the time indicated by the arrow. Product B is being sold according to plan, product A is ahead of forecast, and product C is behind schedule.

C   A work schedule

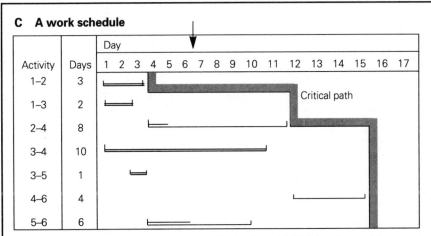

Activity	Days	Day (1–17)
1–2	3	
1–3	2	
2–4	8	
3–4	10	
3–5	1	
4–6	4	
5–6	6	

Critical path

Activity 2–4 is behind plan, and lies on the critical path, so highlighting the need for urgent remedial action.

D   An example of a machine load chart

Machine no.	Mon.	Tues.	Wed.	Thurs.	Fri.
472	* ⊣s⊢	⊣s⊢			
903	⊢	⊣s⊢	* ⊣s⊢		
701	⊢	⊣s⊢		⊢ * ⊣	
703	⊢⊣		⊢ ⊣s⊢		⊢⊣s⊢*⊣

* represents passage of one work task through the schedule
s represents machine setting-up time

Your Management Action

Exercises

Draw up the following activity scheduling charts:

1. Progress chart of getting ready to move house;

2. Work schedule for the summer's gardening programme;

3. Load chart for a conference.

Further reading

Burbidge, J.L. *The Principles of Production Control,* 2nd edn, Macdonald and Evans, London, 1967.

Drucker, P.F. *Management: Tasks, Responsibilities, Practices,* Heinemann, London, 1974.

Lockyer, K.G. *An Introduction to Critical Path Analysis,* 3rd edn, Pitman, London, 1969.

Wild, R. *Production and Operations Management: Principles and Techniques,* Holt, Rinehart and Winston, Eastbourne, 1980.

And finally . . .

The most common form of activity scheduling, seen in almost every workplace, whether office, shop, surgery or workshop, is the holiday rota. Coloured pins, stickers, crayons show when staff members are going to be away.

27 Comparing performance with plan

Much has been made in this book about the need to set goals and objectives. But the reality is rarely going to be quite as things are planned. What is useful for all employees, not just managers, is to have some indication of where performance is differing from the plan so they can adjust their behaviour where and when necessary.

In recent years great efforts have been made in many organizations to deal with quality. This has involved various mechanisms to indicate where there is a difference between performance and plan. For example, quality circles involve those most closely associated with an activity in examining where things are going wrong. The detailed procedures which lead to BS5750 recognition can be invoked where there is something wrong. But how do we know when things are going wrong?

If managers are to be able to compare performance with plans, targets must be set not only in connection with the performance levels expected but also for the nature and frequency of measures to be taken and for the amount of acceptable deviation from plan for each of these measures.

Once performance levels are known to be outside the set acceptable standards, the manager must take decisions on the appropriate remedial action. Factors to be taken into account will include the reasons for the deviation; whether this is due to chance or some other uncontrollable variable such as the weather or a whim of fashion, or whether it is due to inferior/superior performance in any area, thus indicating the need for a change in the input balance. Positive deviations should not, of course, be excluded from detailed examination. Departures from targeted performance levels may indicate a need for fuller explanation of the job, reassignment of duties, better training, additional staffing, more effective leadership or a redrawing of plans or modification of goals.

Some feedback and control mechanisms are automatic and self-regulating. The thermostat on the boiler and the automatic stock re-ordering system are examples of measures being taken, relayed and acted upon immediately and without human intervention. Not all performance is as easily measurable as this, however. For example, feelings that the organization is failing to attract and keep the right calibre of workforce or that the marketing department is not keeping up with fashion are at first sight difficult to measure. The existence of quantified objectives and a well-thought-out control system in all the organization's activities, whether in marketing, production, research, finance or personnel, will assist managers in the process of comparing performance to plan, even in those areas where measurement is less easy to quantify.

Criteria for the setting of controls

Operational and procedural controls only come into effect when events need to be constrained in order to follow plans. They are checks and balances to make sure the system is functioning smoothly and to the correct standards.

According to Drucker *(1974)* they should be:

Economic   Controls exist for an economic, not a moral purpose. They apply to the work of the organization; not to the workers. Their use should be minimized and confined to those occasions when it is necessary to examine the workings of the system.

Appropriate   Energy should be put where it matters. Use the 80/20 rule: this states that, for example, 80 per cent of product costs are incurred by only 20 per cent of all items. Only in the important areas should highly rigorous control procedures be implemented.

Realistic   Controls should always relate to objectives; they should never measure trivial facts, and should never convey false accuracy or carry unnecessary precision. For example, a measure of up or down may be more significant than a specific figure correct to four decimal places.

Simple   Complicated measures only confuse and misdirect energy away from what is being controlled to the control mechanism itself.

Timely   Frequent measurement should be taken, or rapid feedback used, only when absolutely necessary. For example, the evaluation of stock procedures requires a more instant feedback than do research activities.

Operational   The results of control measures should be passed in an appropriate and understandable format, to all those with authority and responsibility to act. This does not necessarily mean top management, but rather shopfloor and office workers, supervisors and first line management.

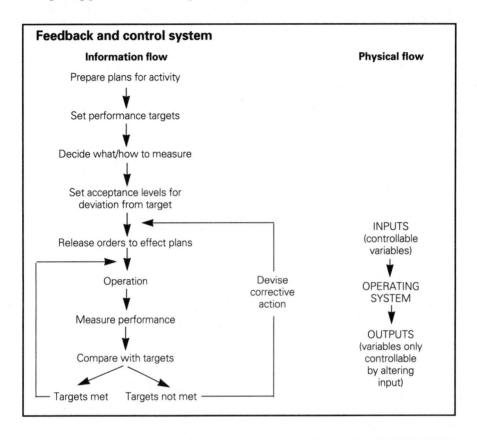

Feedback and control system

Information flow   **Physical flow**

Prepare plans for activity

↓

Set performance targets

↓

Decide what/how to measure

↓

Set acceptance levels for
deviation from target

↓

Release orders to effect plans

Operation   Devise
                            corrective
                             action

Measure performance

Compare with targets

Targets met   Targets not met

INPUTS
(controllable
variables)

↓

OPERATING
SYSTEM

↓

OUTPUTS
(variables only
controllable
by altering
input)

Some conventional control systems

Control area	Objectives of control (these should be as precisely defined as possible)	Feedback devices
Sales	To achieve forecast sales levels	Sales reports
Production	To maximize the efficiency of the work system	Reports of amounts of work in progress, proportion of orders completed on time and resource utilization
Stocks	To establish and maintain optimum stock levels at minimum cost	Reports on stock turnround time, number of stock-out occasions
Budgets	To keep expenditure and profits within required limits	Reports on expenditure and receipts
Personnel	To maximize personal and organizational performance	Appraisal reports and management by objectives, team briefing

Your Management Action

Exercises

1. Imagine that you have decided to rationalize the procedure for the requisition of office equipment in your department. Devise an implementation plan to include your objectives, the performance targets you are seeking and the acceptable deviations, and the monitoring methods you intend to use during the early and later months of the operation of the new system.

2. Note down all the formal and informal control systems used in your department. Do you feel they should be used more/less rigorously? Why?

3. How much feedback do you give to and receive from your superiors? How much do you give to and receive from your subordinates? Consider ways in which you might improve the flow of information both upwards and downwards.

Further reading

Burbidge, J.L. *The Principles of Production Control*, 2nd edn, Macdonald & Evans, London, 1968.

Collard R. *Total Quality: Success through People*, Institute of Personnel Management, London, 1989.

Drucker, P.F. *Management Tasks, Responsibilities, Practices*, Heinemann, London, 1974.

Goldsmith, W. and Clutterbuck, D. *The Winning Streak*, Weidenfeld and Nicolson, London, 1984.

Townsend, R. *Further Up the Organisation*, Michael Joseph, London, 1984.

And finally . . .

Goldsmith and Clutterbuck found that a common factor of control in successful companies was constant feedback of results. Feedback to employees at all levels regarding output and performance gives them tools for self-measurement and self-direction. It provides them with the facts, not just judgements expressed in terms of praise or rebuke. Employees should be treated as concerned adults: bad or contentious news should be passed on as well as success stories, and questions should be answered directly and honestly. Team briefing should include a progress report related to both local and organizational objectives. The open passage of feedback both up and down the line is likely to generate a great deal of useful information.

28   Forecasting trends

Predictions may often lay the foundation for a company's entire business plan. Poor forecasting or the inappropriate application of forecasts will lead to wasted investment in stock, plant, equipment, materials and labour, and to lost revenue due to either forced cost cutting activities or out-of-stock situations.

Most forecasting activities rely on a formal analysis of past data to predict the future. Underlying movements of data over the years are identified and projected into the future, using methods of varying degrees of sophistication and complexity. The more unstable supply and demand movements are, the more important and more difficult accurate forecasting becomes, and the more elaborate the procedures need to be. Even though many of the techniques will be left to the company analysts or computer experts, it is important that managers have an understanding of them, so that they are aware both of the limitations of current methods and of the existence of other, perhaps better, methods. There will be many occasions also on which managers will choose to reject rigid rules and procedures in favour of a more entrepreneurial approach.

The main objective of forecasting techniques is to bring together all information and judgements relating to the problem in a logical, unbiased and systematic way. Where data are scare, qualitative analysis will need to be used. In most cases, however, a combination of both qualitative and quantitative techniques is desirable. It is often of positive benefit to view the same problem from several different approaches. For example, when analysing sales trends, managers can consult sales representatives, hold a conference of experts, and carry out a series of statistical analyses. The results of these various exercises can then be compared and, if appropriate, combined.

The value of using trend analysis and other prediction techniques within an organization goes beyond their technical value, as they provide an agenda for discussion between managers. The organization's future is given a shape by the predictions, and that *possible* shape is one that will focus managerial debate about whether it is the shape they want and how they can alter it.

Prediction of what might happen is, of course, only the first step in the forecasting process. Decisions have to be made as to how to secure the resources needed to accommodate the predicted outcomes, and to ensure that the objectives set in the light of these estimates are met in the years ahead. It is important, therefore, that predictions are as realistic as possible.

Trend analysis and prediction techniques

1. **Quantitative**   Data gathered for past periods are analysed to find out what may have affected the results.

(a) *Time series analysis*

A time series is any set of figures relating to the changing value of a variable over time.

A time series will usually have some or all of the following features:

- Seasonal variations

  Regular, annually repeated movements due to the effect of the seasons on the variable.

- Cyclical variations

  Regular, long-term patterns such as economic boom/depressions or product life cycles.

- Period variations

  Movements in data due to the days of the week in the period or the number of weekends.

- A trend

  An overall tendency for values to rise, fall or remain static.

- Random variations

  Irregular fluctuations in values which fit no other pattern.

These variations are isolated, and their effect separated from the data using various statistical techniques, such as moving averages, exponential smoothing, cumulative sum methods, standard deviations, etc. The data are thus presented in a re-adjusted fashion so that the true movement of the figures is revealed.

(b) *Associative indicators*

There are often relationships which exist between sets of data which can provide some indication of the extent to which knowledge of the value of one variable is useful for the prediction of the value of another. However, it should be remembered that although statistical analysis may show a positive relationship between two sets of data, this is not proof that one has caused the other.

These relationships are identified by statistical methods such as correlation and regression analysis.

Trend analysis and prediction techniques continued

2. **Qualitative** Opinions and judgements regarding predictions and trends are sought from well informed experts, from within and outside the company.

(a) *The Delphi technique* (consulting the 'oracle')
Selected individuals are asked about their estimates and assumptions by means of a questionnaire, often very precise and detailed. Their written responses are coordinated into a 'consensus' view. This is then returned to the individuals with a request to maintain, modify and justify their original judgements. The process is continued, with no contact between the experts, until the considered, personal opinion of each one coincides to form one viewpoint.

(b) *Panel consensus*

Selected experts meet to discuss the issue and to arrive at a group view. The interplay of ideas is encouraged and the method relies on the assumption that cooperation between several people will give rise to a more accurate analysis than that offered by the isolated individual.

Obstacles to the use of trend analysis techniques

In his investigations of technological forecasting practice, Freeman (1982) found that organizations that could have benefited from formal prediction techniques often did not use them. He found that the obstacles to their use were due frequently to lack of management commitment, and included the following:

1. Failure to integrate forecasting activities as a whole into the organization's regular planning programme.

2. Failure to be objective in planning – advocacy and political debate used instead.

3. Failure to understand and welcome analysis techniques.

4. Failure by top management to support forecasting efforts.

5. Failure of management to look into the long term.

Your Management Action

Exercises

1. Think of a forecasting problem in your organization. Note down which elements of the problem would be suited to (a) quantitative and (b) qualitative analysis.

2. Find out how much trend analysis and prediction activity takes place in your own department, and in other departments. Is it formally organized? If so, how is it organized? If not, can you pinpoint the reasons?

3. To what extent are computer programs used in your organization for trend analysis activities? Do you know what software is available in the market to aid managers in these tasks? Find out, if you do not know.

Further reading

Bee, R. and F. *Management Information Systems and Statistics*, London, Institute of Personnel Management, 1990.

Freeman, C. *The Economics of Industrial Innovation*, 2nd edn., London, Frances Pinter, 1982.

Georgeoff, D.M. and Murdick, R.G. 'Manager's Guide to Forecasting', *Harvard Business Review*, January–February, 1986, pp. 110-22.

And finally . . .

An important question to be asked before sophisticated trend analysis and prediction exercises are undertaken is whether the time and effort expended in the process is worth the benefits gained. Where decisions are of a short-term nature and can be changed or reversed with little or no expense, a simple cost/benefit review might indicate that an intelligent guess would serve the purpose quite adequately. On the other hand, decisions which are long term or expensive to change justify the devotion of resources.

29 Graphs and diagrams

Most of us are able to see spatial relationships more clearly than numerical relationships. If you find yourself with a lot of figures to compare, you might start by putting them into some sort of tabular order. Turning the data into pictures may be a further improvement still, particularly if you are looking at comparative trends or proportions. Visual presentation may provide you with a summary as a basis for discussion or may serve simply to clarify a situation in your own mind.

Your audience may feel, with some justification, that you can prove anything you wish with statistics. You should avoid overwhelming people with a vast amount of complex pictures, therefore. Use visual presentation of statistics, not primarily as illumination, but as support for your case in the form of intelligent backup to written or oral argument or demonstration.

Visual presentation methods can be divided into two main groups: *graphs* and *diagrams*. The former is the representation of data by means of a continuous line set within two axes, whilst the latter includes many different forms of visual representation, including bar charts, pie charts and pictorial representation. Whichever method you choose may well depend on personal preference. There are obviously some media which are more suited to certain forms. For example, pie charts are useful for the simple presentation of a large number of component percentages but are little use for showing the increase in volume in aggregated data; bar charts are useful for depicting values in up to four individual components, since the height and length of each bar is proportionate to the magnitudes represented; pictograms present an elementary, yet attractive, form of visual representation useful for presenting changes in total data to a relatively uninformed and undemanding audience; graphs, on the other hand, are frequently used for displaying trends over long periods of time since each point of time occupies relatively little space.

There are many refinements to these basic kinds of statistical presentation which can be used to illustrate specific phenomena, such as frequency distributions, inequalities and relativities. Most basic statistics textbooks describe them in some detail. It is better, however, to use the basic methods competently and accurately than to misuse the more complex methods.

Whether you are a journalist or an advertising copywriter, a speaker at a conference or a report writer, and whether the information you are seeking to present concerns earnings, market growth, geographical distribution, demand levels, percentage population or profit margins, you will probably find your task made easier by the selective use of a graph or diagram. As well as providing instant visual impact to the presentation of comparisons, trends, growth patterns, etc., a diagram in a company report will provide respite for the reader's eye whilst a graphical representation on an overhead projector will offer the viewer a welcome break from concentrated listening.

Simple principles of graph construction

1. A good presentation will be well-defined and undistorted and, therefore, will seek to give an accurate picture of the information. Figure 2 makes a modest rise of 10 per cent in costs look like a disaster. Those who wish to win arguments, to amaze or alarm the viewer or to sell an idea may resort to this tactic. However, if you genuinely wish to convey information, stick to the method used in Figure 1: start your vertical scale with zero and show all the scale points.
   If you really do not have enough space, make it clear that there is a definite break in the scale (as shown in Figure 3).

2. Make it clear what the graph is representing (units, time scales, etc.). Give it a clear title and label both axes or, while people try to work out exactly what is being put across, you will have defeated the purpose of choosing a visual representation.

3. Independent variables (those unaffected by changes in the other variable, e.g. month, year, age) should be placed on the horizontal axis.

4. Make all the lines distinct. Use colours or differently drawn lines (e.g. dotted) where there are several lines. The thickness of the line is unlikely to matter: if accurate values are needed, the original data can still be referred to.

5. Limit the number of lines on one display to avoid confusion or loss of visual clarity.

6. Give the source of data so that details of figures can be obtained, or write the actual figure on the graph itself.

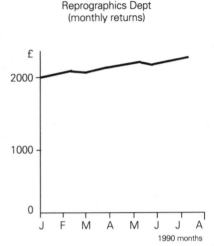

Figure 1
Paper consumption costs
Reprographics Dept
(monthly returns)

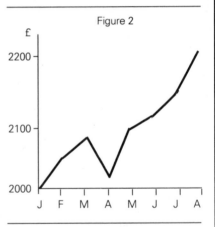

Figure 2

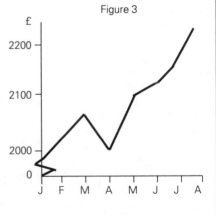

Figure 3

Simple principles of bar chart construction

1. Keep the widths of bars constant, otherwise the volume of the bar will be difficult to compare and the meaning lost.

2. See also the principles for graph construction (but note that the 'break to zero' should never be used in bar charts since it is the correct impression of volume that is important).

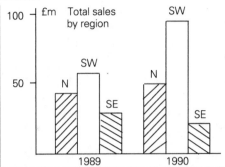

Simple principles of pie chart construction

1. Each segment of the circle is proportional to the size of the figure represented.

2. To construct a pie chart, calculate the angles at the centre of the 'pie' by multiplying each percentage component by 360 degrees (e.g. if one component is 20 per cent of the total figure, the angle at the centre is $^{20}/_{100}$ x 360 = 72 degrees).
   Division can thus be drawn easily with the use of a calculator and a protractor.

3. Limit the number of components shown to seven or eight.

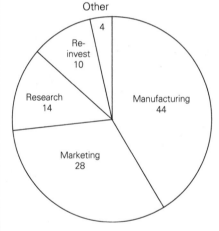

Simple principles of pictogram construction

1. Comparative values are represented by variation in the size or number of objects.

2. Use of a varying number of pictures of the same size is preferable to using one drawing of different sizes. With the latter, there may be confusion over whether it is height or width that is being read, e.g. a doubling in height usually involves a doubling in width also, which may appear as a quadrupling of volume (or an increase by a factor of eight with a three-dimentional picture).

Your Management Action

Exercises

1. In the first six months of 1984, averages for exports to main markets were as follows (in £ million): EEC 138, Australia 122, USA 46, Africa 8, Others 61. Construct a pie chart to represent these figures.

2. Plot both sets of figures, relating to sunshine and profits on suntan lotion, on the same graph using a double scale, one on the left vertical axis and one on the right. Choose scales which result in the two curves occupying similar parts of the graph, e.g. sunshine 0–8 hrs, profits £0–1000.

Period	1	2	3	4	5	6	7	8	9	10
Sunshine (hours per day)	6.1	7.3	6.5	5.8	4.9	4.1	5.5	8.0	7.3	6.8
Profits (£)	621	740	894	773	702	591	488	661	992	863

3. Depict the data below in the form of a component bar chart:

    Subjects studied at the Commercial College, 1990
    (numbers of students):

    *   Professional 1230, comprising Accounting 910, Banking 212, Management 108.
    *   Languages 572, comprising French 302, German 245, Italian 25.
    *   Academic 441, comprising O levels 332, A levels 93, degrees 16.

Further reading

Harper, W.M. *Statistics*, 4th edn, Macdonald and Evans, Plymouth, 1982.
Huff, D. *How to Lie with Statistics*, Penguin, Harmondsworth, 1973.
Yeomans, K.A. *Introducing Statistics*, Penguin, Harmondsworth, 1968.

And finally . . .

Of course, new technology has the ability instantly to convert numerical data into pictures at the flick of a switch. Search through any microcomputer software catalogue and you will find a program which allows you to select a picture type and which will display the chosen graphic on screen using data supplied. The same data can, for example, be transformed into pie charts, vertical or horizontal bar charts or graphs, by the use of just one business graphics software package.

30 Sampling methods

Sampling is taking examples of events, objects or people to represent the whole. Probably the best known samples are opinion polls where one thousand people are asked their political opinions and the newspapers then claim Labour have X per cent, Conservatives Y per cent and the others Z per cent of the vote. It is important that the sample is a reasonable representation of the whole population so that the results can be generalized. Sampling is necessary when it is impracticable to measure, test, talk with or describe every event, object or person. This may be because of lack of time, shortage of money or because the process is continuous whereas the measurement is discrete.

Sampling is a useful method for managers in a variety of tasks. Managers in marketing and sales departments will use it to test new products and advertising campaigns on a sample of the population before committing a large budget. Service industries, including public sector organizations, will sample their clients to see if the public are satisfied and, if not, where the problems exist; personnel departments may sample the employees for their opinions on whether to upgrade the staff restaurant or the sports facilities; work study departments will sample the working practices to identify difficulties; quality control will sample the production, whether batch or continuous, to identify whether the product is up to standard; technical services will take samples of the problem product to take away for analysis, and so forth.

Statisticians call the whole group the population, or universe, and the proportion of this is called the sample. The validity of this sample can be biased in either of two ways. First, by including examples that are not part of the population, for example, the marketing department may test a new cat food advertisement on someone who does not own a cat; or technical services might take a sample for analysis from the batch that is not giving problems. Secondly, the sample can be biased by not being representative of the population. For instance using the telephone directory to sample the population about health services does not include the views of those without telephones, largely the less well off; or if quality control sample a manufacturing process only after lunch, it will not indicate whether the goods are equally well made throughout the day.

There are no upper or lower limits to a sample size. Where statistical techniques are used they may set a minimum number. Otherwise, it is the amount of work and expense that can be justified, since both increase with sample size and yet each extra member of the sample has less impact than the previous one. So a judgement has to be made as to the most appropriate sample size. It helps to ask the all-important question, 'What are the consequences if this sample is an incorrect representation of the whole?' The more critical accuracy is, the greater the expense in time and money is justified and so the larger the sample can be.

Sampling methods

Random sample   selected by pure chance from the population.
1. Number each event, person or period of time.
2. Toss a coin or take every tenth one or pull a name from a hat or look at random figure tables or computer generated figures.
3. Measure, ask, test, those whose number comes up.

Test: Does every name or thing in the whole group have an equal chance to be in the sample?

Examples: Using random figure tables to determine which objects are taken from the production line for testing; giving every tenth guest a questionnaire to complete on hotel facilities and service.

Quota or stratified sample   selected to fit a particular description.
1. List the characteristics of the whole population, particularly as they would affect the issue to be sampled.
2. Decide how many you can afford to sample.
3. Make sure that each of the characteristics is represented in similar proportions to the population.
4. Measure, test, ask those who fit the criteria.

Test: Is your description of the whole population accurate; particularly with reference to the current issue?

Examples: Taking the first, twentieth and last examples from the production line after each process for quality control; market researchers making sure they have 5 twenty-year-olds, 5 thirty-year-olds, and so on.

Bellwether sample   a known sub-set that represents the population closely.

1. Look at previous samples and the results they gave.
2. Select the most accurate sample.
3. Ensure the present purpose is similar and that nothing much has changed since last time.
4. Measure, ask, test the same sample.

Test: Has the population changed since the previous sampling?

Examples: Take sample from production at 3pm as that is when problems usually arise. The viewing panel, who are the sample on which viewing figures are based for television, is a carefully selected cross-section of the public used to ascertain popularity ratings.

Sampling error

Various statistical techniques have been developed to test the likelihood of the sample being significantly different from the population. These tests can be used only where the measurement, descriptions, tests and opinions are numerically recorded.

If sufficient examples of an event, behaviour or process are measured and the results plotted on a graph the shape of the curve tends towards the normal distribution curve. Various mathematical laws are known about this curve. An important one is that $66^2/_3$ per cent of the population is within 1 SD of the mean, 95 per cent within 2 SD and $99^3/_4$ per cent within 3 SD. (SD = standard deviation – a measure of how spread out the curve is from the mean or average.)

The formula for calculating a SD is $\sqrt{\dfrac{(\epsilon x - \bar{x})^2}{n}}$

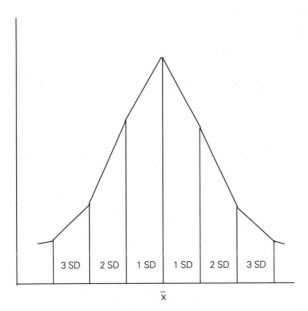

By comparing the results from the sample with the known laws of normal curves a test is made of whether there is a significant difference between the sample and the population. That is, can the results be relied on as representing the whole group?

There are a wide range of statistical tests available, each with particular characteristics suitable for certain circumstances. 't' tests are widely used for a variety of sample sizes, to test whether there is a statistically significant difference between the sample and the population. The particular formulae will vary with sample size and type of measure used. χ^2 is used for comparing an observed set of values with what might be expected and whether there is a statistically significant difference between them. The formulae for χ^2 varies depending on how many things are compared. The formulae for 't' tests and χ^2 will be found in any statistical book or computer statistics programme.

Your Management Action

Exercises

1. If you wanted to know how people voted in the last election, which of the following methods would be most appropriate and why: ask all householders at their doors; telephone everyone listed in the telephone book; telephone every other one; knock on every other householder's door; describe population in terms of age, sex, income, type of house and find proportionate samples; randomly interview those listed on the electoral roll?

2. A chemical plant works on a continual process. When is it most cost effective to take quality assurance samples? What factors need to be considered?

Further reading

Harper, W.M. *Statistics*, 4th edn, Macdonald and Evans, Plymouth, 1982.
Huff, D. *How to Lie with Statistics*, Penguin, Harmondsworth, 1954.
Rees, N. *Eavesdropping*, Unwin Hyman, Hemel Hempstead, 1981.
Robson, E. *Experiment, Design and Statistics in Psychology*, Penguin, Harmondsworth, 1973.

And finally . . .

Samples that are not carefully selected can lead to nonsense. For example, overheard remarks can be amusing, precisely because they are not a true sample of the conversation. Standing on their own, these statements acquire unintended meanings. Nigel Rees has collected some of these, where the context is impossible to fathom:

> *When I do it I tend to catch my fingers on the floorboards. (p. 14)*

> *There are only two in the whole of Guildford and one is covered with ants. (p. 21)*

Perhaps we should always pay attention to De Bono who made the comparison that statistics are like a lamppost to a drunk man. More for support than illumination.

31 Personnel indicators

In this section of the book we have a series of methods for monitoring organizational performance. They are mainly statistical and other measures, but we describe here some general indicators that give early warning of matters which may be affecting employee effectiveness. The two broad categories of indicator are the *survey* and the *trend*. The survey is an attempt to understand some aspect of what is happening in the here and now, while the trend is a regular monitoring of how indicators are changing week by week or month by month through the accumulation and analysis of a large number of frequent incidents.

Some surveys are of demographic data, like the distribution of employees' ages, their sex, racial and ethnic origin, and length of service. In very large undertakings this information may be substantial enough to warrant trend analyses, but usually the data are considered periodically by managers to check the satisfactoriness of the manpower profile. Is there an adequate distribution of ages across the range of jobs, or is remedial action needed to prevent a shortage at some future stage? Is there any indication that women or members of minority groups are being blocked at promotion points?

The attitude survey is a deliberate attempt to find out employee attitudes to features of the business and its management. These have never been widely used and they present problems, such as the discovery of widespread dissatisfaction on some matter which the management feels unable to meet. Would it have been wiser not to open that particular 'can of worms'? Attitude surveys can be useful, but they raise expectations. Also some employees suspect such questioning and may not be prepared to provide the answers.

The main trends to be monitored are absence and turnover. Out of a normal 250 working days in a year, employees are likely to be absent for between 10 per cent and 30 per cent of that time, for authorized or unauthorized absence. Both have to be monitored. One organization has given us the following average figures for its employees over 12 months:

- Annual holiday   20 days
- Training and education   5 days
- Miscellaneous authorized (funerals, jury duty, etc.)   2 days
- Sickness and other absence   9 days

These need to be monitored individually to ensure that the sickness absence is genuine and the annual holiday arrangements do not leave a department unable to operate, but they also need to be monitored for the trends, which then can be compared between departments and for the same period in the previous year. With the relatively tight labour market of the present time, turnover or wastage is not as big a problem as it used to be, and some employers feel that their turnover level is too low rather than too high. It still remains a useful general indicator. Absence and turnover levels can be compared also with published figures, in the Department of Employment *Gazette* and the *General Household Survey*, which provide information on the general characteristics of different regions and industries.

Measuring absence 1: lost time

This shows the percentage of working time that has been lost through employee absence over a given period of time.

$$\frac{\text{Number of days lost through absence}}{\text{Average number of employees x number of days}} \times 100$$

Example: In a workforce of 80, two people are absent for one whole day each and 10 are absent for half a day each, over a period of five days.

$$\frac{7}{80 \times 5} \times 100 = 1.75\%$$

Measuring absence 2: frequency

This shows the extent of the absence across the workforce by showing the number of times people are absent. This can be a useful refinement as frequent short absences can be a bigger problem than rarer long spells.

$$\frac{\text{Number of absences}}{\text{Average number of employees}} \times 10$$

Example: Using the same figures as in the first example,

$$\frac{12}{80} \times 100 = 15\%$$

Measuring turnover 1: separation

The number of people leaving the organization or department is shown as a percentage of the total establishment.

$$\frac{\text{Number of leavers}}{\text{Number of employees}} \times 100$$

Example: Over a period, 85 people leave from a workforce of 300.

$$\frac{85}{300} \times 100 = 28.3\%$$

Measuring turnover 2: stability

As many of those who leave organizations do so in the early weeks of employment, it can be useful to measure the underlying stability by using the formula

$$\frac{\text{Number of employees with more than 12 months' service}}{\text{Average number of employees}} \times 100$$

Attitude survey

Questions in an attitude survey need to be related to current practice in the organization and on matters about which the management needs information. Here are some general questions that might be a starting point for developing a more precise survey. Respondents are asked to tick one of the columns against each statement.

	strongly agree	agree	no opinion	disagree	strongly disagree
Management treatment of employees is fair					
Managers have a firm grip on operations					
If you have a problem you can rely on the departmental manager to get something done					
Employees' views are seldom considered by management when changes are being made					
The work I have to do is generally interesting and satisfying					
I find the atmosphere in my department a pleasant one to work in					
The equipment and materials we have to work with are efficient and well-maintained					
Rates of pay here are better than in most other companies nearby					
Pay differentials between departments are not fair					
I would work harder if there was an incentive scheme					
The company is generally doing well at the moment					
We are well-trained for the work we have to do					
There are good opportunities for promotion					

Any attitude survey should be piloted before use. A sample of the proposed respondents should be asked not only to answer the questions, but to comment on those they could not understand, did not trust or were not willing to answer. They may also suggest additional points to be included.

If people are asked to take part in a survey like this, they will expect to hear something of the outcome.

Your Management Action

Exercise

There are 175 employees in a large office. Over an eight-week period individual employees are absent as follows:

	week 1	week 2	week 3	week 4	week 5	week 6	week 7	week 8
Absent 5 days	3	3	3	4	4	2	2	2
Absent 4 days	1	0	1	2	0	0	1	0
Absent 3 days	4	4	5	5	6	6	8	9
Absent 2 days	7	8	9	9	9	9	9	10
Absent 1 day	9	7	8	9	9	11	11	10
Absent ½ day	5	6	6	7	8	8	9	9
Absent 1 day twice	2	2	1	0	1	2	3	2
Absent ½ day twice	2	2	2	4	0	0	3	3
Absent ½ day three times	1	0	0	0	0	2	2	3
Absent 1 day once, ½ day once	2	4	0	4	3	4	4	5

Calculate the lost time for each week and the frequency for each week. How do these calculations improve your understanding of the position?

Further reading

Advisory, Conciliation and Arbitration Service, *Labour Turnover*, Advisory Booklet No. 4, ACAS, London, 1984.
Advisory, Conciliation and Arbitration Service, *Absence*, Advisory Booklet No. 5, ACAS, London, 1984.
Central Statistical Office, *Social Trends*, HMSO, London, published annually.
Department of Employment, *Gazette*, HMSO, London, published monthly.

And finally . . .

The following statements are generally valid:

1. *Younger employees have more short spells of absence than older employees; older employees are more likely to be off for long periods.*
2. *Except for maternity leave, there is little difference in the amount of sickness absence taken by men and women until the later years of employment when men are likely to lose more time.*
3. *Manual employees are more likely to be absent from work than white-collar employees.*
4. *Among those with degree-level qualifications under the age of 35, turnover among men is higher than among women.*
5. *Absence is highest among those working shifts, heavy overtime and in large working groups.*

32 Managing consultants

Managers' relations with consultants have a peculiar love/hate quality. Consultants have to be used, yet they are regarded with deep suspicion. The attitude towards the relationship is further complicated by the fact that many managers increasingly adopt a consultancy mode of operating inside their own organizations at the same time as using external consultancy services themselves. This is a particularly strong feature of the personnel role, and the personnel manager who cannot perform the consultancy role skilfully is in danger of having only a peripheral role in organizational affairs. The personnel manager who cannot commission effective external experts, who are well-briefed and productive, is in danger of losing even a peripheral role.

There are some activities that are undoubtedly best undertaken by consultants. An example is the use of psychological tests in selection. This is partly because only the largest organizations recruit on a scale significant enough to make comparative analysis worthwhile in developing some sort of vocational norms. Few employers can accumulate the volume of data needed to make useful predictions, but consultants who specialize in selection can establish large banks of test result data acquired from applicants to a wide range of organizations.

Another widespread use of consultants is in training, the logic being that specialized trainers are often needed, yet it is too expensive for an organization to maintain these experts on the full-time payroll.

The difficulty managers have with consultants is partly one of credibility and partly one of control. There are so many people operating as consultants that it is difficult to know who to pick, but also many managers feel that using consultants indicates a lack of expertise or confidence by the manager. Confident and competent managers can call in outside experts without fear of jeopardizing their own position and can specify closely what they require. Where a manager lacks professional expertise, then consultants will be used reluctantly, with a poor specification of requirements and the likelihood of an unsatisfactory outcome for both client and consultant. Briefing a consultant to provide what you need rather than what the consultant wants to provide requires great care. Subsequently monitoring what the consultant does so that you get what you need requires even greater care.

Using a consultant is not an easy option: it requires considerable input and thought from the briefing manager.

The Preying Mantis
Of all the businesses, by far,
Consultancy's the most bizarre.
For, to the penetrating eye,
There's no apparent reason why,
With no more assets than a pen,
This group of personable men
Can sell to clients more than twice
The same ridiculous advice,
Or find, in such a rich profusion,
Problems to fit their own solution.

The strategy that they pursue –
To give advice instead of do –
Keeps their fingers on the pulses
Without recourse to stomach ulcers,
And brings them monetary gain,
Without a modicum of pain.
The wretched object of their quest,
Reduced to cardiac arrest,
Is left alone to implement
The asinine report they've sent.
Meanwhile the analysts have gone
Back to client number one,
Who desperately needs their aid
To tidy up the mess they made.
And on and on – ad infinitum –
The masochistic clients invite 'em.
Until the merciful reliever
Invokes the company receiver.

No one really seems to know
The rate at which consultants grow,
By some amoeba-like division?
Or chemo-biologic fission?
They clone themselves without an end
Along their exponential trend.

(Windle, 1985)

Seven reasons for using consultants

(1) To provide specialist expertise and wider knowledge not available within the client organization. (2) To provide an independent view. (3) To act as a catalyst. (4) To provide extra resources to meet temporary requirements.
(5) To help develop a consensus when there are divided views. (6) To demonstrate to employees the impartiality/objectivity of personnel changes or decisions. (7) To justify potentially unpleasant decisions.

(Wood, 1982, p. 41)

Briefing a consultant

1. *Describe the problem* What is the issue about which you might seek outside help? This may not be obvious, as worrying about an issue can show that the real matter needing to be addressed is not what is immediately apparent.

2. *Formulate an approach* Work out a rough approach to the problem, with the emphasis here on 'rough'. You need something clear but not inflexible, so that you can go through the remaining stages of making up your mind without putting the consultant, and yourself, in the wrong framework.

3. *Work out how you could deal with the problem in-house* How could it be tackled by using your own existing resources, how much would it cost, how long would it take and what would the repercussions be, such as stopping work on something else?

4. *Find out how it could be done by consultants* Invite one or two potential outside suppliers of expertise, to bid for the business on the basis of stages 1 and 2.

5. *Decide between the alternatives* Compare relative costs, times and likely outputs, as well as implications, remembering that the responsibility is inescapably yours.

Changing someone else's behaviour

A is the consultant, B is the person who has to do things differently:

1. A perceives a problem. A will not be able to wait for B to see the problem, so it will have to be pointed out, either by a simple statement or by producing persuasive evidence. A must not, however, suggest that B is the problem, nor should B perceive A as the problem!

2. B takes responsibility for finding solutions to the problem, but realizes that A could be a useful source of ideas.

3. A and B evaluate alternatives and their implications. As B now sees A as a potential source of help the alternatives can be evaluated to make sure that a change is likely to be an improvement, rather than simply different.

4. B decides on an alternative that A can accept. The responsibility for making and implementing the decision remains with B, even though it will need to be acceptable to A; it does not have to be ideal.

5. B tries the changed method and A provides support, help and reassurance. The early stages will be the time of greatest difficulty for B and the time for a positive contribution from A. It is not helpful if A disclaims responsibility or joins the critics.

6. B either consolidates the change in behaviour or abandons it in favour of another. A may also be abandoned if seen as the source of unhelpful advice. (Based on Leavitt, *1972.)*

Your Management Action

Exercises

1. Identify three knotty problems facing your organization generally or you in your job:

    - Which would you remit to a consultant? Why?
    - How would you specify what you want the consultant to do?
    - Which would you not remit to a consultant? Why not?

2. With the problem that you are not sending to a consultant, formulate an approach to solving it using the '5 W–H' method (Priestley et al., *1978*):

    - What is the problem?
    - Who is involved?
    - Where is worst?
    - When is worst?
    - Why does it happen?
    - How could it be tackled?

Further reading

Leavitt, H.J. *Managerial Psychology*, 3rd edn, University of Chicago Press, Chicago, 1972.

Priestley, P., *et al., Social Skills and Personal Problem Solving*, Tavistock, London, 1978.

Windle, R. *The Bottom Line*, Century-Hutchinson, London, 1985.

Wood, D. 'The Uses and Abuses of Personnel Consultants', *Personnel Management*, October, 1982.

And finally . . .

Interviewing for consultants:

> *(1) Listen to what the person being interviewed is saying. Listening also implies not talking too much. In assessment the interviewer should not be talking for more than 10 per cent of the time.*
>
> *(2) Be courteous. One good way of doing this is to treat interviewees as though they were slightly more intelligent, slightly older, possibly of the opposite sex, and of a slightly higher status than yourself . . . unless, of course, you encounter someone who actually fulfills all these conditions: the best thing to do in those circumstances is to try to treat such a person as an equal.*
>
> *(3) Be confident. You are not on show and are just doing your job to the best of your ability.*
>
> *(Priestley et al., 1978, p. 181.)*

Part D

Managing people

33 Organizing the department or section

Chapters 12 to 17 dealt with the main questions of organization structure; this section examines how individual departments are organized. This is partly determined by the overall structure and philosophy of the organization. Individual employees, however, often find their greatest frustration at the level of the department rather than the undertaking as a whole. Also, many of the exciting new developments that companies plan get into difficulty at the departmental level, through ineffective co-ordination of what individual employees and groups of employees actually do.

The work of people in departments is co-ordinated by various methods, the first being mutual adjustment, which is informal communication between a small group of people, like a family running a grocery or a pair of labourers fitting double-glazing. In a slightly larger unit there will be supervision, whereby one person is responsible for the work of a number of others, like the captain of an aircraft. A third method of co-ordination is to standardize the work to varying degrees. Automation is the extreme example, but most people work within some standardization, like the drills for administrative action described in Chapter 23. Slightly different is the standardization of output, as in the specification to the skilled worker of the requirement, such as repairing a leaky valve, rather than specifying how the work should be done. The final method of co-ordination is to standardize skills; the close-knit social organization of the hospital operating theatre is largely achieved by the diverse skills of the individual team members, whose professional training then specifies their contribution. Most medical teams can work efficiently together even without knowing each other, because of this knowledge of the role that accompanies each skill.

The basis for departmentation in a business is seldom clearly thought out, and new departments are constantly being created to meet an assumed need or to satisfy the career aspirations of an individual. A systems department, for example, may be set up because there is the emerging function of data processing that needs specialist expertise. Otherwise there will be differing systems, inappropriate equipment specified, and general inefficiency. It is easy to set up the new department, but what other departments then need to be discontinued or have part of their function removed? These questions are seldom asked. Similarly a new department may be created to give accelerated experience to some promising young executive who has to be blooded for major responsibility in a few years' time, but what may become redundant elsewhere in the organization as a result of that innovation?

We suggest below a five-stage process for either organizing a department from scratch or for identifying problems of organization in a long-standing department.

Five steps in departmental or section organization

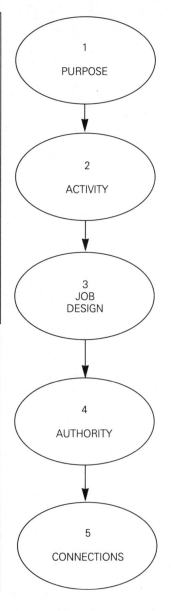

Step 1 What purpose will the department serve in the organization?

- Is the purpose of the department to meet a basic business objective, like sales or purchasing, or is it in the hope that the organization will run more smoothly, like personnel? If the latter, where are the savings to justify the innovation?

- Has the new department been set up on the basis of outputs, like business objectives to be achieved, or is it based on inputs, like people and problems? If the latter, can outputs be produced to justify its existence? Are those outputs already being produced elsewhere in the organization?

- Is the new department to deal with something that senior managers do not understand, like new pensions legislation, or something they find unattractive, like negotiating with trade union officials? If the answer is 'yes', are the reasons good enough?

- Will the new department make problems of inter-departmental communication and coordination fewer or greater?

Step 2 What activities can be identified that will enable the department to meet its purpose?

- Is the department grouping together those who share a particular skill, like word processor operating, or a particular responsibility, like quality assurance?

- What are the activities to be carried out to meet the department's purpose? How many people with what types of experience and qualification are needed to undertake those activities?

- How many ancillary employees, like errand boys and typists, are needed? How can that number be reduced? How can it be reduced further still?

- Are all the identified activities necessary? What do they take away from other departments? Will there be duplication? Is there a better way? Is the new department really needed?

Step 3 **How are the activities of the department best grouped into jobs?** (see also Chapter 34)

- How much specialization is needed? Can some jobs be made more satisfying for the job holder by reducing the amount of specialization and increasing variety? Will that impair or enhance departmental efficiency? What degree of specialization is needed to maximize expertise without making the department too dependent on irreplaceable hyper-specialists?

- Are boundaries between jobs clearly defined, or will there be arguments about who does what?

- Will job holders have sufficient discretion to carry tasks through to completion, or will they be waiting constantly for other people and for decisions from others on matters they can satisfactorily resolve themselves?

Step 4 **What formal authority do the job holders need delegated to them?**

- Are there job descriptions or other labels that indicate the authority that the job holder has to operate? Are there ways in which the labelling can authorize more effectively?

- Do all job holders have the necessary equipment, like keys, and information, or computer codes, to carry out their duties within the department effectively?

- Do all job holders have the necessary authorizations, like written permissions and authority to sign documents, that are needed for effective working in relation to other departments?

- Are there any restrictions on the authority and autonomy of junior members of the department that exist only to provide symbolic status to senior members? If so, are they needed?

Step 5 **How can the activities of job holders be connected through information systems and reporting?**

- How do job holders know what they need to know about the activities of their colleagues? Are there enough meetings to be informative but not so many that they become tiresome? Are there enough copies of memoranda and wastepaper baskets big enough to cope with them after they have been read, so that only essential material is filed? Are the possibilities of electronic mail fully utilized?

- Is the physical location of individuals such as to aid communication between those who are constantly exchanging information?

- Is there the best possible drill for routing papers and other material undergoing transformation by department members?

- Is information that is withheld from job holders done so of necessity?

Your Management Action

Exercises

1.   What is the purpose of your department and would that purpose be met better if there were more or fewer activities covered by it?

   Think about how you answered that question. Were any of the activities that you wanted to add included because you thought their addition would enhance your personal status or career prospects? If so, would their addition also improve the working of the entire organization? If their addition would not improve the working of the entire organization, how would your personal status and career prospects be affected? Were any of the activities you wanted to shed included because you find them boring or difficult? If so, what are the implications of their being moved elsewhere?

2.   What features of the way your job is connected to others make you most dissatisfied? In the light of your answer, are there aspects of how your subordinates' jobs are interconnected that you will now modify?

3.   If you have a private office, how much practical benefit does that confer apart from the satisfaction of privacy? If you do not have a private office, what benefits would you envisage from such a privilege? To what extent are your answers real and to what extent are they rationalizations?

Further reading

Child, J. *Organization*, 2nd edn, Harper and Row, London, 1984.
Wild, R. *Work Organization*, John Wiley, London, 1975.

And finally . . .

No department is very effective without good informal integration. The pensions department of a large business had on one occasion to send out 3500 letters to employees. This was a tedious, routine job and it took a great deal of time because the details on each letter had to be carefully checked. Usually work of this nature is passed down to the most humble member of staff, who resents the imposition, takes a long time over the job and makes mistakes. In this company all members of the department did it, working in the last half hour of the day every day for a week.

Not only was the job done quickly, it was done thoroughly. When there were subsequent enquiries from recipients of the letter, all members of the department could cope quickly with a range of questions through having had to understand completely the letter and all its implications. They had also been socially integrated by sharing in a single task, where they were all on an equal footing.

34   Job design

Who designed your job? You will probably say that it was not designed at all: it just exists. Most jobs have developed over quite a long period and in two different ways. First, there is general development, so that sales assistant jobs have come into existence to meet broadly similar demands in different places and selling different things. Jobs like mechanic, typist, machinist, clerk, driver, managing director or ballet dancer all have similar characteristics or core elements. Secondly, there is the way a job has been developed, and sometimes designed, in a particular situation, so that the job of coach driver has similar general characteristics in the local bus company as with an international tour operator, but the specific features of the two jobs are very different. Differences between similar jobs affect recruitment, training, payment and effectiveness. Few of those ideally suited to drive the school bus every morning would be as well suited to the same basic driving job, taking tourists to Turkey, and seldom would the same people apply for both jobs.

Job design is the process of getting the optimum fit between the organizational requirements from the individual employee and the individual's needs for satisfaction in doing the job. Because there are more jobs to be altered than thought out from scratch, it is sometimes described as *job redesign*.

Initially the management approach to job design was to make things as simple as possible for the employee to increase productive efficiency, following the theory that the simpler the task the quicker it could be completed. The extreme form of this idea was in mass production assembly lines where the complete task for an employee could be completed in as little as 45 to 60 seconds, with the same task being repeated 400 or 500 times a day. Increases in productive efficiency were impressive, but so were the increases in labour turnover, absenteeism, dissatisfaction, alienation, industrial action, sabotage and mental illness.

Attempts to mitigate the ill effects on employees were first concentrated only on the context of the work, such as the nature of supervision, the use of rest periods and attention to the ergonomic aspects of the workplace. Since 1959 initiatives have been made to alter the content of jobs, with great interest in how the nature of the job itself can motivate the job holder. To demonstrate success investigators have taken existing jobs and changed or redesigned them in order to compare performance before and after the change.

It is more practical to look at job design as the logical step to follow departmental organizaton. The third step of departmental organization suggested in the last chapter was 'How are the activities of the department best grouped into jobs?' By asking that question it is possible to design jobs that are coherent and whole, avoiding the artificial specialization that comes from merely making things simple. Job wholeness can produce departmental efficiency, economical staffing and satisfied employees.

Two well-known approaches to job redesign

1. *Job enlargement* extends the scope of jobs by combining two or more jobs into one, or by taking a number of work functions and putting them together in a single job with an increased variety and wholeness. The expansion is horizontal.

2. *Job enrichment* is a method that gives people more responsibility to set their own pace, decide their own methods and put right their own mistakes, so increasing their autonomy. The expansion is vertical.

Job redesign is no panacea

The design of jobs has to be logical for organizational reasons as well as being an attempt to improve the lot of the employee. Enriched or enlarged jobs will motivate only those who seek personal fulfilment through work. That search, and the commitment that goes with it, will be directed towards the job only if the employee can see prospects of real personal growth by that means. The job that is made much better than it was still may not have enough potential for employees to seek fulfilment through work: they may continue to seek it outside work.

The American sociologist Harry Braverman *(1974)* believes that the labour process of the twentieth century has moved the planning and design of work tasks so irrevocably away from the employee and towards management that no change is possible without workers resuming control of their own work. If workers directed their own work it would not be possible to 'enforce upon them either the methodological efficiency or the working pace desired by capital'. The large-scale rationalization and de-skilling of first manual work, then clerical work and more recently management work through the computer, has removed skill, responsibility and control from the employee.

Few escape

Job design is not only an activity directed to the rank and file employee. A research study of management in American companies well known for management development included the comment:

> management in the typical organization was characterized by having rather narrow jobs and very tightly written job descriptions that almost seemed designed to take the newness, conflict, and challenge out of the job.

Job dimensions and their effects

1. *Skill variety*   The way a job demands a variety of different activities that involve using a number of different skills and talents.

2. *Task identity*   The way a job requires the job holder to complete a whole and coherent piece of work having a tangible outcome.

3. *Task significance*   The way a job has an impact on the lives or work of other people, inside the organization or outside.

} These give meaning to the work people do

4. *Autonomy*   The way a job holder enjoys freedom from supervision, independence and discretion in deciding how the job should be done.

} This gives responsibility to job holders

5. *Feedback*   The way the job holder receives clear and direct information about his effectiveness.

} This gives the job holder knowledge of results

Ways of getting good results on the five job dimensions

ACTION	JOB DIMENSION Affected
(a) *Forming natural work units* so that the work to be done has a logic and makes sense to the job holder.	2, 3
(b) *Combining tasks* so that a number of natural work units may be put together to make a bigger and more coherent job.	1,2
(c) *Establishing links with clients* so that the job holder has contact with the people using the service or product the job holder is supplying.	1, 4, 5
(d) *Vertical loading* so that job holders take on more of the management of their jobs in deciding what to do, organizing their own time, solving their own problems and controlling their own costs.	4
(e) *Opening feedback channels* so that job holders can discover more about how they are doing and whether their performance is improving or deteriorating.	5

(Based on Hackman, *1987.*)

Your Management Action

Exercises

1. Consider the job you now hold and think of ways in which it could be redesigned in terms of the five job dimensions listed earlier.

   (a) Which of those changes would *adversely* affect the work of someone else?

   (b) Which of the changes would *adversely* affect organizational efficiency?

   (c) Can those adverse effects be mitigated, or are there different changes to make that will avoid them?

   (d) What is stopping you from initiating the changes?

   (e) How and when are you going to tackle the problems that prevent you from redesigning your job?

2. Draw up an organization chart or network of the kind of business you have always wanted to set up, concentrating on how the work to be done would be divided up into jobs rather than concentrating on reporting relationships.

   (a) How would you alter those jobs in line with the five job dimensions?

   (b) How many jobs have you lost/added?

   (c) Will your wage/salary bill be higher or lower?

   (d) Would you enjoy running the business more or less as a result of the changes?

   (e) Are you more or less likely to gamble your life savings by starting up the business?

Further reading

Braverman, H. *Labor and Monopoly Capitalism*, Monthly Review Press, New York, 1974.

Hackman, J.R. 'Work Design', in Steers, R.M. and Porter, L.W. (eds) *Motivation and Work Behaviour*, 4th edn, McGraw-Hill, Maidenhead, 1987.

Smith, J.M. and Robertson, I.T. *Motivation and Job Design*, Institute of Personnel Management, London, 1985.

And finally . . .

Work banishes the three great evils of boredom, vice and poverty.

(Voltaire, Candide, 1738)

35 Understanding other people

We all need to understand other people so we can make friends, understand our families and influence others. The last of these is one of the main tasks of management, to influence other people to do things they would not do otherwise. This persuasion can be through coercion or eliciting willing co-operation. By understanding more about how other people view things, what interests them, what they see as important, the more likely we are to choose appropriate ways of influencing their behaviours towards our preferred outcome. This may be by overt manipulation of the reward system or ensuring rapport is so good that the other person's view is thoroughly explored, finding something for them in what we require, or selecting the argument that the other person will find most convincing. The aim is for the interests of both parties to be sufficiently well served for there to be mutual satisfaction. To do this we need to understand how things look from the other person's point of view. However, seeing things from the other's perspective is extremely difficult. This can be helped by understanding more about the nature of individual differences and so increasing our effectiveness when working with a variety of people.

The variety of the human race is due to each of us having a unique combination of genes and experiences; even identical twins have a different set of experiences. These different combinations give us our individual ways of behaving and thinking that we call our personality. Philosophers, theologians, psychologists and others argue over the relative influence of 'nature', genes and 'nurture', upbringing, on our personality. Some, like Freud, argue that we have deep-seated irrational and impulsive instincts, modified by acquired moral values. Others, such as Skinner, emphasize that our current behaviour is learned by experience and that we are more likely to repeat behaviours that have been rewarded in the past.

Each of us operates with assumptions about why people do particular things. By making these assumptions explicit, and realizing that we work with a particular model, we will find it easier to understand that other people may be operating with an entirely different viewpoint. We all assume that behaviour is to some extent controlled and not random. We believe that people are seeking, consciously or not, to attain certain goals.

There are lots of formal, psychological models of human behaviour that can help at work. We can look at different models of human beings and theories of motivation to help us understand customers, suppliers, other managers, subordinates or the boss. Each theory is partially accurate but only partly explains the mysteries and complexities of human behaviour. The day we can wholly account for individual variations is the day our behaviour will become as predictable as that of robots. This may make management more efficient but will be far less fun for human beings.

Perception

This is the term used to describe the process of selecting, organizing and interpreting incoming stimulation. We all do it differently and so perceive a different 'real' world. To most people it seems ridiculous to discuss the way one perceives the world because the 'real' world is so familiar and stable. This constancy and stability is to do with our mental processes, as the actual visual or other sensory input is constantly changing. This section looks at some of the reasons why people perceive the same situation differently.

1. The obvious difference in *physical sensitivity*. Human organs are sensitive to only a limited range of things. For example, none of us can see x-rays. Some people are more or less sensitive than others, for example partial sight or hearing makes a difference to the stimulation received.

2. *Selective attention*. We attend to some things and ignore others. For example, at a party we can concentrate on one conversation and ignore others: we focus on what is important to us. If, however, someone says our name, we usually hear it even in a conversation we are not part of.

3. *Categorize the cues* as they come in. The incoming stimulation is fitted to one of our preexisting schemata. Schemata are the categories we have, made up of concepts, ideas and associations built up in our memory as a result of our experience. This process may well be influenced by language.

4. There is a *limit* to how much we can categorize at any one time. This is not just a limit by how much is coming in but also the ease with which we can categorize the stimulation. The time when we feel most overwhelmed at work is when lots of difficult communications are coming to us. Whereas the office party, when there are probably just as many communications but easier to categorize and decide what action is required, is nothing like as overwhelming.

5. *Context and expectation* often determine the kind of categorization we make. If we are expecting to see our colleague at the airport it is surprising how often we misidentify someone else before we meet our colleague. Whereas if we meet the same colleague accidently in the supermarket it may take us a little while to remember their name.

6. Our *attitudes and personality* will influence what we perceive. They generate expectations. A prejudiced person sees the behaviour of those they are prejudiced against in a negative way whatever actually happens. A friendly act will be seen as false, a casual approach as sloppy, a remote stance as difficult and so on. This in turn will affect the behaviour of the perceiver and you get the beginnings of self-fulfilment.

    The act of perceiving is a constructive process where we make sense of our environment by trying to make it fit our experience. The real world is different for each of us, as we perceive it differently.

Motivation theories

Maslow *(1954)* grouped needs into five stages and contended that only when the needs in the lower stages were satisfied did the next stage become potent. Once a need was satisfied it was no longer a motivation although it could return later.

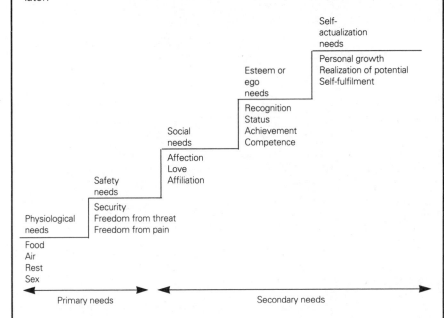

Herzberg *(1968)* developed this hierarchy as it affects the motivation of people at work. Hygiene factors lead to dissatisfaction if they are not up to standard but increases above this do not give more satisfaction. In contrast the satisfiers can motivate beyond the basic level as people want more of these regardless of how much they have.

Hygiene factors	Satisfiers
Company policy and administration	Achievement
Supervision	Recognition
Working conditions	Work itself
Salary	Responsibility
Relationship with peers	Advancement
Personal life	Growth
Relationship with subordinates	
Status	
Security	

It should be noted that both these writers researched among middle-class Americans. Not everyone agrees that they can be applied across time and space universally. However, there has been a continuing popularity for both models in the UK among managers on a 'felt useful' basis.

Your Management Action

Exercises

1. What criteria would you use to distinguish between understanding the needs of a fellow worker and indulging them?

2. List five factors that the interviewer is looking for in an employment interview. Now do the same thing for the interviewee. Do these two viewpoints have anything in common?

3. What assumptions do you make about those you work with? Does this fit with any of Schein's models?

Further reading

Herzberg, F. 'One More Time: How do you Motivate Employees?' *Harvard Business Review*, Jan./Feb., 1968.

McGregor, D. *The Human Side of Enterprise*, McGraw-Hill, New York, 1960.

Maslow, A.H. *Motivation and Personality*, Harper and Row, New York, 1954.

Schein, E.H. *Organizational Psychology*, 3rd edn, Prentice Hall, Englewood Cliffs, New Jersey, 1980.

Zalkind, S.S. and Costello, T.W. 'Perception: Some Recent Research and Implications for Administrators', *Administrative Science Quarterly*, no. 7, pp. 218-235, 1962.

And finally . . .

Zalkind and Costello suggest the following for improving the accuracy of one's ability to understand other people.

1. *The better we know ourselves, the easier it is to see others accurately.*

2. *One's own personality affects what one sees in others.*

3. *The accuracy of our understanding depends on our sensitivity to differences in people.*

36 Power and authority

Power is an inescapable part of management. One of the main purposes of organizational charts is to describe the formal allocation of power to job titles. Organizational politics is the use of power in organizations. It involves any activity that seeks to acquire, develop and use power and other resources to ensure a particular outcome where various options are possible.

If there were always total agreement about objectives and how to achieve them there would be no need to change or influence other people. The very nature of organizations, with their variety of individuals, groups and interests, inevitably leads to conflict. There is conflict over the priority of objectives and the use of resources. So power is an important attribute and the use of that power is political action. Many meetings within organizations are convened with the main purpose of resolving the conflict between two groups, for example the relative responsibilities of the day and night shift; maintenance and production schedules; the use of the conference room.

Power is the ability to influence others to do things they would not have done otherwise; authority is the possession of legitimate power. Power does not exist on its own, but as some part of a relationship. You can have power over others only if you have something they want. So power is part of a dependent relationship. It is also two-faced; it is central to the process of social integration, but it divides people through the emergence and development of conflict over who has, or should have, power.

The dimensions of these power relationships can be described in various ways. Magnitude refers to the amount of power a person or group has; for example, does the stock manager control all the materials others need? Distribution is whether power is widely dispersed, or concentrated in a few hands; can the materials be released by anyone in the stock office or only by the boss? Scope describes the range of activities over which the powerful has control; does the stock manager have power to control the budgets for purchasing new stock? The domain of power is the degree to which it extends from one relationship to another; the stock manager may be powerful when requests for materials are concerned but powerless when plans for future reorganizations are made.

To have authority is to have legitimate power, unless one takes the most nihilistic or anarchistic view that no power can be legitimate. This process of legitimizing is one of the features that distinguishes organizations from mobs. We can distinguish two types of authority; to be *in* authority or to be *an* authority. *In* authority is the position or title which permits the holder to have power over others. Carter *(1979)* discusses how this authority is dependent on other sources of power, for example control of resources, to maintain itself. Being *an* authority is having the skill, knowledge and expertise that others consult without compulsion. The surprise is that more managers do not try to develop an expertise of their own, as the basis of their authority, to support their positions of power.

Techniques used to obtain power

Technique	Benefit to self and organization	Drawback for self and organization
Alliances Collaborate with others where interests are sufficiently similar	Have someone on your side; their resources and skills	Degree of commitment; not easy to discard, as a discarded ally becomes an enemy
Lobby Get support from others on particular issues		
Doing favours Provide services, support, information, materials and expect reciprocation		If done too much, others become suspicious
Being present at meeting or conference where important decision is taken	Interest is heard; you are involved in decision-making	Time consuming
Cornering resources Gathering people and materials into one's own area	Number of staff and size of budget can be measured, unlike most management activities	Empire-building is not necessarily related to organization's objective
Being indispensable Either through expertise or by being an essential part of the administrative process	Can become an authority	Can become obsolete
Reciprocal support for patron Having a 'god-father' in a powerful position	Better to be pulled up the hierarchy than to push oneself up	Patron likely to exact fealty
Being able to cope with uncertainty Those who have expertise to deal with crises such as mending the machine or seeing a way round the problem		Only powerful in crises, so crises may be created

(Sources of power are discussed in Chapter 1.)

The importance of organizational politics to the manager

1. It helps to influence what and how something is done.

2. Members of organizations have to compete with each other for resources and to develop their careers.

3. As management performance is difficult to measure, building areas of influence is an alternative way of showing one's ability.

4. There is an increase in political activity when decisions are taken by committees, task groups and alliances, rather than by individual managers.

5. Favourable job mobility within an organization requires political awareness.

6. Organizations operate in a political context, due to international events, government policies and the activities of competitors.

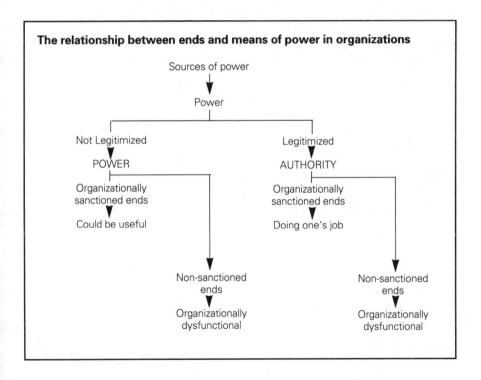

The relationship between ends and means of power in organizations

Your Management Action

Exercises

1. Which techniques for gaining power have you used? Which have you found effective?

2. Make a list of the various parts of your job. Which of these has a political slant? Which would you consider to be non-political? Which do you spend time worrying over?

3. Think of examples for each of the four outcomes in the figure above.

4. Is it possible that the final outcome of authority used for non-sanctioned ends could be organizationally functional?

Further reading

Carter, A. *Authority and Democracy*, Routledge and Kegan Paul, London, 1979.

Dahl, R.A. 'Power' in *International Encyclopedia of the Social Sciences*, Vol. 12, pp. 405–15, Macmillan, London, 1968.

Duverger, M. *The Study of Politics*, Nelson, London, 1972.

Jay, A. *Management and Machiavelli*, Penguin, Harmondsworth, 1967.

Machiavelli, N. *The Prince*, Penguin, Harmondsworth, 1981.

Pfeffer, J. *Power in Organisations*, Pitman, London, 1981.

Snow, C.P. *The Corridors of Power*, Penguin, Harmondsworth, 1963.

Snow, C.P. *The Masters*, Penguin, Harmondsworth, 1963.

And finally . . .

The only purpose for which power can be rightly exercised over any member of a civilised community, against his will, is to prevent harm to others. His own good, either physical or moral, is not a sufficient warrant.

(*J.S. Mill*, On Liberty, *1859*)

The graveyards of history are strewn with the corpses of reformers who failed utterly to reform anything, of revolutionaries who failed to win power . . . of anti-revolutionaries who failed to prevent a revolution – men and women who failed not only because of the forces arrayed against them but because the pictures in their minds about power and influence were simplistic and inaccurate.

(*Dahl, 1968, p. 15*)

37   Staff selection

Few managers are able to pick their own teams of staff. They have to work with the people who are there when they are appointed and may later appoint one or two more people to fill vacancies as they develop, or to cope with expansion. Most managers are, therefore, occasional selectors only and will be more concerned with whether or not a prospective new recruit will fit in with the established staff team than with whether or not the person is the best equipped in other ways. Personnel specialists are more likely to steer the short-listing and preliminary interview stages, with the departmental manager coming in at the end to decide on the potential fit between appointee and existing team members.

The departmental manager can therefore assume that some form of job description will have been produced so that applicants are applying for something that they understand and feel able to do. There will also be some form of candidate specification or profile of the sort of experience, qualifications and other characteristics needed in applicants. Those two should eliminate unsuitable applicants so that the manager is left with the question about who is more suitable than others.

For each applicant there will be an application form or curriculum vitae (CV), or both. Forms have the advantage of providing the same categories of information for each candidate in the same way, so that comparisons are easy. This is especially useful in short-listing a large number of applicants. CVs allow the candidate to choose the method of presentation and determine the content, so that there is probably more information about that particular individual.

In some organizations there will be test scores available for candidates before final selection. Managers need to guard against the temptation of interpreting these scores as 'good' or 'bad', but should take advice about their interpretation, and the weight to be placed upon them, from the personnel specialists who administered them. The use of written references appears to be slightly increasing; they have always been used extensively in the public sector of employment, and their use is now slightly higher elsewhere. You need to be sure what questions have been asked of the reference writer and what is his or her knowledge of the work of the person about whom the reference is written.

You now have to interview the applicant, to decide about the potential 'fit'. The best guide for the interview will be either the application form or the CV, as both provide a structure for questioning to expand the information already provided. Use the interview to obtain information and develop your understanding of the candidate; leave making decisions until later. The best known guide for decision-making in selection is the seven-point plan devised by Alec Rodger (1952). Overleaf, there is an alternative suggestion, together with suggestions about conducting the interview.

The four 'don'ts' of selection interviewing

Research has shown that the following are the most common faults of selection interviewing. Each of them can be eliminated by the person who understands the danger and uses just a little self-discipline.

1. *Don't* make up your mind on the basis of first impressions and then spend the rest of the interview looking for evidence to prove you are right; you could be wrong. Use the interview to obtain information and then make up your mind.

2. *Don't* betray any tentative judgement you may have during the interview itself. Candidates will react to what they think your tentative opinions are and either try to alter them or become taciturn because they think they have failed the test.

3. *Don't* rely on the general impression the candidate gives: look for evidence relevant to the vacancy.

4. *Don't* look for reasons why the candidate will not do: look for the reasons why she or he could do the job.

Making selection decisions

J. M. Fraser *(1978)* has devised a fivefold framework for selection decisions. Use the form below to organize your thinking about candidates, marking A, B, C, D or E in each box, with A meaning much above average declining to E, signifying much below average.

	Candidates			
	1	2	3	4
1. *Impact on others,* or the kind of response a person's appearance, speech and manner call out from others				
2. *Qualifications and experience,* or the skill and knowledge required for different jobs				
3. *Innate abilities,* or how quickly and accurately a person's mind works				
4. *Motivation,* or the kind of work that appeals to an individual and how much effort he or she is prepared to apply to it				
5. *Emotional adjustment,* or the amount of stress involved in living and working with other people				

Conducting a selection interview

1. *Opening*   Seat the candidate comfortably and then 'tune in' to each other by inconsequential discussion about the weather or a similar neutral subject. Explain what is to happen and offer plenty of smiles and nods. Relaxed candidates are more informative than terrified ones.

2. *Information exchange*   Move to a more businesslike pace to obtain information and answer questions. Use a logical sequence for the interview, such as going through the stages of the working record. Use an opening question that will be easy to answer and informative, like 'Can you give me an outline of your present duties?' Concentrate on enabling the candidate to be frank and informative. Check key points from the application form that need clarifying.

3. *Listen to the candidate*   at all times, make notes, control the interview.

4. *Closing*   Explain what happens next. Check that the candidate has no more questions.

5. *Review job and candidate information*   Read through: job description, candidate specification, application form, interview notes, references (if any) and test scores (if any). Decide whether or not the candidate fits the job and the implications of any poor fitting.

6. *Decide between candidates*   Complete a fivefold grading form (see above) for all candidates who fit the job. Consider how each would fit the relevant working group. Guard against unlawful discrimination. Decide to whom the offer should be made and on what terms.

References

References, especially character references, are notoriously unreliable. When reading them, remember:

1. Look for the substantive and explicit comments.

2. Do not 'read between the lines' as you may see a message that is not there.

3. Look for the recommendation. There are a number of much-used phrases, such as
    'I recommend without hesitation . . .'
    'I recommend for serious consideration . . .'
    'Well worth considering . . .'
    'Ready in many ways for promotion . . .'

Your Management Action

Exercises

1. Write a reference for an anonymous person applying for your job, without making it over-enthusiastic or damning. Then show it to a friend and ask if he or she would be likely to employ the person or not, with reasons. What does this tell you about the use of references? How will you modify your reading, and writing, of references in the future?

2. Use the form on the previous page to make a decision about a position contested by four candidates. Use a job and people you know, like four members of the cabinet who might aspire to be prime minister, or four of your subordinates who might be interested in your job. Is the answer you produce by this method different from your initial snap judgement or assumption? What has caused the difference?

3. Use the interview guide on the previous page to give someone interview practice.

Further reading

Fraser, J.M. *Employment Interviewing*, 5th edn, Macdonald and Evans, London, 1978.
Lewis, C. *Employee Selection*, Hutchinson, London, 1985.
Rodger, A. *The Seven Point Plan*, National Institute for Industrial Psychology, London, 1952.
Torrington, D.P. *Management Face to Face*, Prentice-Hall, Hemel Hempstead, 1991.

And finally . . .

Some extracts from references:

> *Mr A is now coping much better with his problems . . .*
>
> *Miss B has not quite fitted in here, but I'm sure that was our fault rather than hers.*
>
> *Mr C has set himself very high standards and has complete faith in his ability eventually to reach them.*
>
> *Mrs D has very neat handwriting and excellent timekeeping. [Mrs D was applying for a senior management post in local government.]*
>
> *Dr E can be a pain, but if you have a sufficient supply of aspirin the pain is probably worth it.*

38 Counselling and coaching

Counselling is not the same as giving advice and coaching is not the same as training; they are complementary aspects of the management art, which develop skill and effectiveness in another person by *not* telling him or her what to do, but by enabling him or her to find solutions to problems and to develop strengths in job performance. Both are typically provided informally and spontaneously as people talk things through and find their way past difficulties by bouncing them off another person, who provides a different perspective, so that the person with the problem develops a more rounded understanding.

Occasionally counselling is done on a more formal basis. A specialized form is redundancy counselling, where those facing redundancy are offered assistance by the employer or by a specialized consultant. The counsel will be sought on the basis that the counsellor has some information or advice to give, but the interview would be ill founded if it did not develop as a session in which those being counselled find their own solutions, and exercise their own responsibility.

Counselling has some common features with the situations of dealing with the poor performer and performance appraisal, which are covered in the next two chapters. The similarity is that neither the counsellor nor the other person know 'the answer' before the interview begins; it is developed by the process of interaction itself.

Coaching is the art of trying to improve the performance of someone who is already competent; training is the skill of bringing someone to a level of competence in the first place. This requires a different type of working relationship, as the coach may not be a better performer, but will have elements of expertise, wisdom and judgement that the other person finds helpful. An example woud be the international tennis professional, who will certainly be able to beat the coach in a match, but may depend on the coach to produce that calibre of performance by guidance, criticism and analysis.

Although closely associated, counselling and coaching are not the same thing:

> The proper object of *coaching* is to improve present performance; the proper job of *counselling* is the realization of potential. The former emphasizes *doing*, the latter *becoming*.
>
> (Lopez, *1968*, p. 112)

Both activities require authority in the counsellor, who must first be in a position to obtain relevant information. Other aspects of the necessary authority are respect for the person being counselled, a familiarity with the coaching/counselling process, and an ability to take up the frame of reference of the other person, so that the matter is discussed from his or her point of view.

Modelling behaviour

In the counselling interview or discussion there is the opportunity for the counsellor to model certain behaviours for the client in order to modify the client's mood. The main examples are:

1. *Calmness* to reduce agitation in the client.

2. *Confidence* to reduce uncertainty and anxiety in the client.

3. *Attentiveness* to increase the likelihood of the client being attentive as the interview proceeds.

4. *Absence of dismay* should the client reveal information about which shame or guilt is felt.

Methods of listening

Counsellors can be effective only if they can listen, which is more than allowing other people to talk and more than hearing what they say. Aspects are:

1. *Willingness* to listen by believing that the client has something to say and making sure that you have understood it, not making any assumptions before the story is complete.

2. *Time* to listen by indicating either that there is an unlimited amount of time, or at least that there is plenty, and not allowing any indication of impatience, like the furtive glance at the wristwatch.

3. *Space* to listen by ensuring that the meeting is private and free from interruption, and that counsellor and client do not have any awkward barriers between them, like desks or long distances.

4. *Attention* to what is being said, by strong focus on the client and the absence of distractions.

Stress inducers

Thomas Holmes, an American psychiatrist, has devised a scale of life incidents that produce varying levels of stress risk. The following are extracts from his list; the higher the points, the greater the risk:

Death of spouse	100	Divorce	73
Death in close family	63	Personal illness	53
Getting married	50	Being dismissed	47
Retirement	45	Pregnancy	40
Large mortgage	30	Responsibility	
Moving house	20	change at work	29

Stages in a counselling interview

Counselling interviews develop in many different ways, and counsellor style, warmth and integrity are more important than technique. Here is a useful sequence to experiment with:

1. *Factual interchange*   Focus on the facts of the situation first. Ask factual questions and provide factual information, like the doctor asking about the location of the pain and other symptoms, rather than demonstrating dismay. This provides a basis for later analysis.

2. *Opinion interchange*   Open the matter up for discussion by asking for the client's opinions and feelings, but not offering any criticism, nor making any decisions. Gradually, the matter is better understood by both counsellor and client.

3. *Joint problem-solving*   Ask the client to analyse the situation described. The client will receive help from the counsellor in questioning and focus, but it must be the client's own analysis, with the counsellor resisting the temptation to produce answers.

4. *Decision-making*   The counsellor helps to generate alternative lines of action for the client to consider and they both share in deciding what to do. Only the client can behave differently, but the counsellor may be able to help a change in behaviour by facilitation.

Mentoring

Mentoring is a form of coaching which reproduces in a modern organization the working relationship of skilled worker and apprentice by attaching a new recruit to an established member to induct, guide, coach and develop the recruit to full competence and performance.

One set of advice for mentors is:

> *M*anage the relationship
> *E*ncourage the protégé
> *N*urture the protégé
> *T*each the protégé
> *O*ffer mutual respect
> *R*espond to the protégé's needs

Your Management Action

Exercises

1. Bartenders are the repository of many confidences as the maudlin unburden themselves late at night. Ask one or two bartenders, early in the evening, about their experiences with sad drunks and how they cope, then see what aspects of method they seem to have in common.

2. The next time you are involved in a conversation with someone who is agitated or upset, try modelling behaviour for them, as suggested on the previous page.

3. The next time you have a serious conversation with another person, try the methods of listening suggested on the previous page.

Further reading

Clutterbuck, D. *Everyone Needs a Mentor*, Institute of Personnel Management, London, 1985.

Lopez, F.M. *Evaluating Employee Performance*, Public Personnel Association, Chicago, Ill., 1968.

Rogers, C.R. *On Becoming a Person*, Houghton Mifflin, Boston, Mass., 1971.

Wright, P.L. and Taylor, D.S. *Improving Leadership Performance*, Prentice-Hall, London, 1985.

And finally . . .

There is always the risk that the client or protégé will become dependent on the counsellor, coach or mentor. Folklore reports that certain famous screen performers are unable to make love convincingly on film without a prior consultation with their analyst. Counselling and coaching can produce similar dependency and many coaches or counsellors find that dependency rather attractive as it boosts their own ego. This is, of course, the worst possible outcome, as the working performance has not been developed and may have been impaired.

39   Dealing with the poor performer

In formal organizations the responsibility of management is to organize the materials and work into suitable chunks, so that properly selected and trained people willingly perform well. But even the best run department will have the occasional poor performance. There may be problems with the materials, the organization of the work, inappropriate selection and training, or idiosyncratic problems. These problems of poor performance may be short or long term, individual or group, a problem of quantity or quality or, *in extremis*, all of them combined. This chapter is mainly concerned with the long-term individual problem, whether of quality or quantity.

Before anything can be done to improve poor performance, it is important to establish that there is a gap between required performance and actual performance. The work expected is communicated formally to members of an organization by contracts of employment, company rule books, job descriptions, training manuals, standards and procedures. Expectations are communicated verbally at meetings and briefing sessions, individually and during training. There may be reasons for poor performance in any of these; they may be out of date, for example, or communicated inadequately to the employee.

To establish what actual performance has taken place there are various sources of information. Some, or all, of these need to be referred to when establishing the gap (see list below). Having checked what is expected and what has been done, the question is whether there is a sufficient gap between the two to need attention.

Having decided that there is a gap between actual and required performance, it is necessary now to establish the reason for it. Personal reasons are those that arise from the employee's personal and family circumstances, and impede performance. This produces the ethical dilemma of to what extent, and for how long, the organization can allow personal problems to interfere with performance. Organizational reasons are those that provide a mismatch between the individual and the particular job, that can be dealt with either by clearer instructions or by transfer to other work. Individual reasons are those where the employee does not fit in with the particular working group or into the organization as a whole.

Having established the reason, or reasons, for the poor performance, ways of dealing with it will suggest themselves. This is best done by setting goals, together with the poor performer, for improvement, discussion of what additional resources will be provided in the way of clear instructions and training, and when the performance will be reviewed. The two previous stages of establishing the gap and finding the reasons for it are important, but only in so far as they serve the main objective of dealing with poor performance: improvement.

Sources of information about the actual performance

- Personalities
- Time sheets
- Sickness and absence records
- Work and record cards
- Others doing similar work to provide comparison
- Unfinished work
- Reject book
- Customer complaints
- Colleagues who come in contact with the individual

A check-list for dealing with the poor performer

Establish the gap: Expected performance   Actual performance
                        Rules communicated   Records
                                                   Average

Reasons for the gap:
- Personal
- Organizational
- Individual

Ways of dealing with it:
- Set goals
- Review them

Reasons for poor performance

Personal characteristics outside the organization's control

- Intellectual ability
- Emotional stability
- Physical ability
- Domestic circumstances
- Family break-up
- Health

Aspects of the organization that are outside the individual's control

- Assignment and job
- Job changed
- Pay
- Poor discipline
- Investment in equipment
- Physical conditions
- Lack of training
- Inappropriate permissiveness
- Planning or improvisation
- Location and transport
- Inappropriate training
- Poor management

Individual reasons arising from a mismatch with the organization.

- Poor understanding of the job
- Sense of fair play abused
- Motivation
- Personality clashes within the group or with superiors
- Inappropriate levels of confidence
- Conflict of religious or moral values
- Group dynamics

Ways of dealing with the poor performer

The following are not given in order of execution but as starting points to assist thinking when a problem arises:

Goal setting
Jointly agree specific reasonable goals and a date to review the performance (see also Chapters 24 and 40).

Training
Make sure you give appropriate training, preferably on the job, so there is no problem in making the connection between the training and the working situation (see also Chapters 42 and 43).

Dissatisfaction
Fill the gap where appropriate; remedy particular problems such as pay or conditions.

Discipline
These range from the informal discussion through to increasingly formal procedures and punishment, ultimately including dismissal (see also Chapter 52).

Reorganizing
Where the problem has arisen through difficulties with the work, materials, reporting relationships, physical arrangements being no longer adequately organized.

Management
Improve the clarity of communicating the task, monitoring systems or the expertise of a particular manager.

Outside agencies
Particularly appropriate where there are personal and family reasons.

The job
Transfer to a more appropriate job or department; redesign the job (see also Chapter 34).

Peer pressure
Where an individual performance is very different from the average those working alongside will feel it inappropriate and may put pressure on the individual to change.

Your Management Action

Exercises

1. Is the punctual, poor worker more or less likely to be reprimanded than the late, good worker at your place of employment? Is your company's procedure reasonable?

2. How would your boss establish a gap between your actual performance and what is expected of you?

3. Do those lowest in the hierarchy get blamed for poor performance more readily than managers because it is easier to establish a gap?

4. What systems are used in your place of employment to monitor quantity and quality of work?

Further reading

Advisory Concilation and Arbitration Service. *Discipline at Work*, ACAS, London, 1987. (Available free.)

Miner, J.B. and Brewer, J.F. 'The management of Ineffective Performance', in Dunnette, M.D. (ed.) *Handbook of Industrial and Organizational Psychology*, Rand McNally, Chicago, Ill., 1976.

Stewart, V. and A. *Managing the Poor Performer*, Gower, Aldershot, 1982.

Video Arts. *So You Think You Can Manage?* Methuen, London, 1984. (Based on the John Cleese films, so popular on management courses, one of which, 'I'd like a word with you', is relevant to this chapter.)

And finally . . .

The 'red hot stove rule' was originally advanced by the American Douglas McGregor, who likened effective discipline to the touching of a red hot stove:

> *(a) The burn is immediate, so there is no question of cause and effect.*
>
> *(b) There was warning; the stove was red hot, and you knew what would happen if you touched it.*
>
> *(c) It is consistent; everyone touching the stove is burned.*
>
> *(d) It is impersonal; you get burned, not because of who you are, but because*
>   *of what you have done.*

40 Performance appraisal

> Performance appraisal is the number one American management problem. It takes the average employee (manager or non-manager) six months to recover from it.
>
> (Peters, *1989*, p. 495)

Schemes of performance appraisal are being introduced and constantly modified in all areas of employment, causing more management frustration than most aspects of management work. Despite the problems the potential advantages are so great that schemes continue to be introduced and the results can be stunning.

Success in appraisal starts with being able to achieve the right attitude in the mind of the appraisee, seeing potential value in the process and having confidence that it will produce results. Ideally the appraisee thinks something like this:

> I would like to talk through with someone how I am getting on and where I am going: my progress, my hopes, my fears. I need to do this with someone who has the experience and wisdom to discuss my performance with me so that I can shape it, building on my strengths to improve the fit between what I can contribute and what the organization needs from me. If appraisal can do that for me, I may then be able to come to terms with my limitations and understand my mistakes.

With that sort of starting point appraisal can have significant effects, for example:

1. Developing co-operative behaviour between appraisers and appraisees, encouraging appraisees to exercise self-discipline and accept responsibility.
2. Difficult issues are confronted and problems resolved.
3. There is searching analysis directly affecting performance.
4. It requires high trust, engenders loyalty and stimulates initiative.

Appraisal works best with people who are professionally self-assured, so that they can both generate constructive criticism and cope with it afterwards. It is based on the assumption that, although they may need support, the only people who can improve the performance of those appraised are the appraisees themselves, and appraisees will achieve only what they believe they can achieve. Appraisers who can be accurate in diagnosis but demoralize the appraisee are themselves in serious need of appraisal.

Who should carry out the appraisal?

1. *Immediate superior*   By far the most common practice is for the superior to appraise the performance of immediate subordinates. It has several of the problems mentioned on the previous page, but it reinforces conventions of responsibility and accountability.

2. *Subordinates*   Logically subordinates are well placed to appraise the performance of their superiors, but it is a rare practice.

3. *Outsiders*   Some schemes use the appraisal of someone out of the line of responsibility, like a management development advisor or an outside consultant, in order to screen out bias. The drawback is that this person will have no direct experience of the appraisee's working performance and will be limited to assessment on the basis of personality traits and the interview.

4. *Assessment centres*   A specialized form of appraisal is to use a group of experts to assess potential through an extended series of activities over several days. This, of course, is concerned only with possible future jobs rather than the existing one.

5. *'Grandfathers'*   Appraisal by immediate superiors is often checked by the superior's superior ('grandfather') before being finalized. This is intended as a check against bias or carelessness.

6. *Oneself*   A number of organizations include an element of self-rating in their schemes on the basis that no-one has greater interest in, nor more knowledge about, the working performance than the person doing the job, so they begin the process by producing their own appraisal, which is either discussed with, or compared with, the appraisal of someone else. This approach requires an organizational setting in which people feel secure and able to analyse their own performance.

From the horse's mouth – comments from Institute of Personnel Management examination scripts

'Our scheme has been abandoned because of a lot of paperwork to be completed by the manager and the time-consuming nature of the preparation by both appraiser and appraisee. Assessment dragged on from week to week without any tangible outcome, there was no follow-up and few people understood the process. The interview was spent with managers talking generalities and appraisees having nothing to say.'
(From a large engineering company)

'We have had approximately one new scheme per year over the last six years. These have ranged from a blank piece of paper to multi-form exercises, complete with tick boxes and a sentence of near death if they were not complete by a specified date.'
(From an international motor manufacturer)

'Our scheme is not objective and has become a meaningless ritual. It is not a system of annual appraisal; it is an annual handicap.'
(From a public corporation)

Maier's three approaches to the appraisal interview

1. *Tell and sell*   The interview is used to tell appraisees the outcome of the appraisal and persuade them of the need to improve in the ways specified.

2. *Tell and listen*   The interview is again used to pass on the outcome of the appraisal, but the reactions of appraisees are carefully checked, and as a result the appraisal is possibly modified.

3. *Problem-solving*   Job problems are discussed openly, much in the manner of a counselling interview, on the assumption that this will enable appraisees to improve job performance through enhanced understanding and the support from the organization subsequently provided.

Typical problems with performance appraisal

- *Paperwork*   Documentation soon gets very cumbersome in the attempts made by scheme designers to ensure consistent reporting.

- *Formality*   Both participants in the interview realize that their meeting is relatively formal, with much hanging on it.

- *Prejudice*   The appraiser may be prejudiced against the appraisee, or anxious not to be prejudiced; either could distort the appraiser's judgement.

- *Insufficient knowledge of the appraisee*   Appraisers sometimes appraise because of their position in the hierarchy rather than because they understand what the appraisee is doing.

- *The 'halo effect'*   The general likability or otherwise of an appraisee can affect the assessment of the work the appraisee does.

- *Context*   The difficulty of distinguishing the work of appraisees from the context in which they work. Is relative ineffectiveness due to personal ineffectiveness or an impossible situation?

- *Outcomes are ignored*   Follow-up action agreed in the interview for management to take fails to take place.

- *Everyone is 'just above average'*   For effectiveness the process has to engender self-confidence in the appraisee. The easiest way for appraisers to ensure this is to state or imply that the appraisee is doing at least as well as most, and better than a good many. It is much harder to deal with the situation of facing someone with the opinion that they are average – who wants to be average?

- *Appraising the wrong features*   Sometimes behaviours other than the real work are evaluated because they are easier to see, such as punctuality, looking busy, sounding keen and being pleasant.

Your Management Action

Exercises

Try this with a close friend. The aim is to talk real stuff about your respective jobs. One of you is *A*, the other is *B*.

1. *A* prepares by writing responses on separate cards to the following questions:
    - (a) An activity you perform in your job that is very important. This should begin with a verb (e.g. 'carrying out appraisal interviews'), not a role or responsibility.
    - (b) An activity you do frequently – not necessarily important, but one which occupies a good deal of time.
    - (c) An important activity, which is unlikely to appear in your diary.
    - (d) What is the most important activity not so far listed?
2. *B* now interviews *A* about the above topics.
    - How are (a) and (b) similar, and how are they different?
    - What makes them easier, or harder, to do than (c)?
    - Which is it more important in your job to do well, (b) or (c)?
    - On what criteria did you select (d)?
    - Which gives you most satisfaction, (a), (b), (c) or (d)?

Now change roles.

Further reading

Maier, N.R.F. *The Appraisal Interview: Three Basic Approaches*, University Associates, La Jolla, California, 1976.
Peters, T. *Thriving on Chaos*, Pan Books, London, 1989.
Torrington, D.P. *Management Face to Face*, Prentice-Hall, Hemel Hempstead, 1991, ch.12.
Wright, P.L. and Taylor, D.S. *Improving Leadership Performance*, Prentice-Hall, Hemel Hempstead, 1984.

And finally . . .

> *I have had annual appraisal for three years. Each time it has been a searching discussion of my objectives and my results. Each interview has set me new challenges and opened up fresh opportunities. Appraisal has given me a sense of achievement and purpose that I had never previously experienced in my working life.*
>
> *(From an insurance company)*

41 Brainstorming

A senior UK management consultant has suggested that 'in any organization and at any level in that organization, there exists a deep, untapped well of useful ideas' (Rawlinson, 1981). However, the very nature of many organizations often militates against the independent, challenging and impulsive approach considered necessary for the production of creative ideas. Therefore, there has grown up a variety of structured aids to creative problem solving in organizations, accompanied by the belief that creativity can be acquired and improved through instruction and practice. One such technique is brainstorming, a name probably derived from the colloquial meaning of brainstorming indicating brainwave.

Brainstorming has been defined simply as a means of getting a large number of ideas from a group of people in a short time. The chief purpose of the activity is to produce a check-list of ideas which gives rise to a new and better solution to a specific problem. This is achieved by overcoming various barriers to creativity.

Many people have a tendency to conform to the methods and conventions expected or practised by colleagues. This may be politically astute, but it inhibits creative thought since it results in a lack of effort in challenging the obvious. There may be an assumption also that where information appears to belong together, the next stage is a foregone conclusion and requires no further thought. The result is an instinctive 'yes' or 'no' before ideas are given a chance to develop. Many ideas are thus buried at the initial stages of the thought process. People also have an excessive faith in reason and logic, and in rejecting these they risk being proved wrong or being made to look fools. The brainstorming session seeks to break down these barriers; to provide an occasion at which remote associations between thoughts and ideas may be invoked and explored to produce solutions which are less stereotyped and more creative than could be obtained otherwise.

It should be remembered that certain problems may not be suited to brainstorming exercises, for example those that are extremely diffuse or complex, or those requiring an extremely high level of specific technical knowledge. However, problems suited to brainstorming activities include the search for new products or markets, trouble-shooting, managerial problems and process improvements. Examples include finding uses for conductive plastic, reducing the amount of pollutants in rivers, improving the company's safety record or reducing fuel costs.

There are two modes of thought, vertical and lateral, which can be applied to such problems. Both have their place, and on the whole neither one should be used to the exclusion of the other when seeking solutions. De Bono points out that, like reverse gear on a car, creativity and lateral thinking are particularly useful when up a blind alley or when manoeuvrability is required.

The brainstorming process

1. Preparation
   Selection of a suitable topic for brainstorming and the participants in the session.

2. Statement of the problem
   The group is given advance notice of the problem in the form of a brief description of one or two sentences. The originator of the session discusses with the group a limited amount of background information relating to the problem, thus introducing it into participants' minds.

3. Warm-up session
   Participants are introduced to the concepts of brainstorming in a relaxed manner. Group discussion aims to identify the barriers to creative thinking and shows how they can be overcome. The actual brainstorming process is explained, together with the four rules of brainstorming: free association, elaboration, suspension of judgement, and speed. A short practice-run demonstrates how little time it takes to produce 50 to 100 ideas.
   At the end of the warm-up session, the original problem is restated in as many ways as possible. For example, the problem of falling turnover could be redefined as how to beat competitors, or how to display better. All restatements are written down by the leader.
   This session should be carried out even for experienced groups. Its purpose is to help participants escape from the pressures and constraints of daily life. It should also develop a lighthearted, easy-going atmosphere.

4. Brainstorm
   The leader/scribe reads out the restatements and calls for ideas. As they flow, they are numbered and written up on a large flipchart with a large felt-tip pen. Each sheet is torn off when full and displayed elsewhere in the room. Noise and laughter should be encouraged. Ideas will flow fast at first and then fluctuate; a short pause can act as a stimulus for more ideas. The ideas may number from 150 to 600, or more. There should be no pre-set timescale for this session.

The brainstorming process, continued

5. **Wildest ideas**
   When ideas really seem to have dried up, the leader closes the session by asking members to select the 'wildest ideas' from the list and turn them into something useful. This may produce yet more ideas, and also leads to the session ending on a high and light-hearted note. No attempt should be made to evaluate yet.

6. **Evaluation**
   This takes place over the next few weeks/months, with the purpose of identifying the few good ideas for implementation and of demonstrating to participants that their efforts were worthwhile. The process involves scrutiny of the ideas, selection of possible winners, and examination against established criteria, such as cost, implementation time, feasibility. The final few are then chosen.

Criteria for selecting participants

Experience of brainstorming	Wide range, to include old and new hands
Background discipline	Widespread, to include outsiders and not just those working in the problem area
Personality	Needs people with constructive attitudes; a good mix of ages and sexes is useful
Company seniority	Wide range – the most senior is not automatically the session leader, but may assist later in the progression of ideas
Inclusion of the expert	Only one member should be categorized as an expert
Group size	Minimum six, maximum 20 (12 is a good number)
Inclusion of observers	No observers allowed, only participants

Your Management Action

Exercises

1. Enquire from your training department whether your organization
    offers any courses in creativity, and put yourself down for one.
2. In the next three months undertake your own self-learning programme
    on creativity techniques, and brainstorming in particular.
3. Talk to your colleagues about brainstorming. Try to identify an
    organizational problem which might be resolved in this manner.
4. Think about your own blocks to creativity, and note down those to
    which you think you should pay the most attention.
5. Set aside 60 to 90 minutes for a warm-up session at work, using the
    following problems as practice runs:
    the noisy dog in the house next door; the large pile of bricks in the yard
    outside your office; the equipment disappearing from the drawing
    office.

Further reading

De Bono, E. *Lateral Thinking for Management*, McGraw-Hill, Maidenhead,
    1971.
Rawlinson, J.G. *Creative Thinking and Brainstorming*, Gower, Aldershot,
    1981.
Rickards, T. *Problem Solving Through Creative Analysis*, Gower, Epping,
    1974.

And finally . . .

*Like any other management technique, brainstorming has to be understood and
practised to be effective. Training should help to remove the mystique
surrounding this method of problem-solving. It is important also that the culture
of the organization is such that a positive and innovative approach to problem-
solving is encouraged among all levels and all departments. The overriding
principle behind brainstorming is that quantity in idea production leads to
quality, so that perhaps one solution only might come out of many hundreds of
ideas and many working hours. Such a process requires the organization's
managers to exercise tolerance, patience and foresight.*

42 Training – instruction

There have been a lot of changes in organizations over the last decade. There has also been an increasing concern about training over this period. Many argue that Britain does not spend enough on training its workforce. So what are the main purposes of training? Tyson and York (*1982*, p. 178) list them as:

1. Maximizing productivity and output.
2. Developing the versatility and employability of human resources.
3. Developing the cohesiveness of the whole organization and its sub-groups.
4. Increasing job satisfaction, motivation and morale.
5. Developing a consciousness of the importance of safety at work and improving standards.
6. Making the best use of available material, resources, equipment, and methods.
7. Standardizing organizational practices and procedures.

Trainers often spend a great deal of time anguishing over what method to use on a training programme. The Training Agency in Britain spends a great deal of money in schools, colleges, universities and other organizations developing particular methods of training. This can become something of an obsession with process at the expense of content. In the past there was probably too much emphasis on what we learn; now there is probably too much emphasis on how we learn. Clearly we need to consider both. A small study of 64 students who were taught in different ways was tested immediately after the session and a month later, and there was no difference in the amount learned by lectures, case studies, role play or other experiential methods. Gale *et al.* (*1982*, p. 16) conclude:

> It appears trainees can learn effectively in a variety of different modes, perhaps indeed finding as much or more satisfaction from *what* they are learning than the *way* in which they are trained.

This suggests we should not become too obsessed with how we learn; it is much more important that what we learn is appropriate. Whatever the content, however, there are some general guidelines about which are easier methods of learning.

This chapter is concerned with one particular sort of training – how to teach someone to carry out a specific task, like wiring a plug or calculating a correlation. The next chapter is about broader aspects of training.

The sequence for learning

Gagne (1975) has identified a chain of eight events that take place whichever sort of learning is involved.

1. *Motivation*   The learner has to want to learn and want to learn this particular thing or the final product of this type of learning.

2. *Perception*   The matter to be learned has to be distinguished from others. This involves identifying a clear objective. At first this is difficult because one has not yet learned the different categories in the area. With time one learns more and more detailed ways of classifying the matter to be learned.

3. *Acquisition*   What has to be learned is related to the familiar so that it makes sense.

4. *Retention*   The two-stage process of human learning comprises short-term memory where items are stored first before being transferred permanently into the long-term memory. Not everything needs to go, or does go, into long-term memory. For example, the anecdotes and jokes that aid the process of understanding at the time need not be transferred to long-term memory.

5. *Recall*   This the ability to summon up from memory when required. There are different levels. Recognition is where we know we have seen the item before and it takes less time than previously to familiarize ourself with it but we could not have used the memory on its own. Recall is where we can independently generate the memory. You might recognize some of the material in this book as something you remember hearing or seeing before; it will seem like 'common sense'. Some other bits you could recall from memory without the book because you have learned them more thoroughly.

6. *Generalization*   This is the ability to apply the learning in settings other than the specific situation that was learned.

7. *Performance*   This is where what has been learned is done. It is the test of the learning.

8. *Feedback on performance*   This where the learner finds out whether the performance has been satisfactory or not. Sometimes this will be obvious because of the quality of the performance, particularly with physical skill learning. But some feedback from the coach or trainer can help to distinguish more suitable levels of satisfaction and analyse what went wrong, how it could be avoided, what needs more practice, what to do next and so on.

Learning can fail because of problems at any of these stages. The careful trainer or coach will run through this list when helping another prepare for learning and when giving feedback at the end of the learning experience.

Techniques for instruction

- **Skill instruction**
  The trainee is told how to do it, shown how to do it, and does it under supervision. This is suitable for communicating skills as long as the task is broken into suitable parts. The breaking down of tasks into suitable parts will vary with the task and the person to receive this training. This form of training is not appropriate for all skills as some tasks are best learned as a whole.

- **On the job**
  Here trainees work in the real environment with support from a skilled person. This gives the trainee real practice and it does not involve expensive new equipment. However, not all skilled people are skilled trainers.

- **Programmed instruction**
  Trainees work at their own pace using a book or computer program which has a series of tasks and tests geared to teaching something systematically. It is suitable for learning logical skills and knowledge. It does not allow discussion with others. This might be important where the application may be debatable.

- **Role play**
  Trainees are asked to act the role they, or someone else, would play at work. It is used particularly for face-to-face situations. It is suitable for near to real life work, where criticism would be useful. The difficulties are that trainees can be embarrassed and the usefulness is very dependent on the quality of the feedback.

- **Exercise**
  Trainees do a particular task, in a particular way, to get a particular result. This is suitable when trainees need practice in following a procedure or formula to reach a required objective. The exercise must be realistic.

Kolb's experiential learning model

This model suggests that the learning process is a cycle of the following stages.

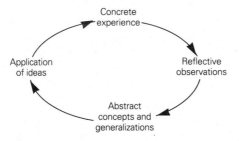

(Source: Kolb et al., 1974)

This is a particularly useful model for devising coaching and learning experiences on the job (see Chapter 39).

Your Management Action

Exercises

1. What have you found difficult to learn recently? Use Gagne's list to analyse where the problem lay.

2. Use the Kolb cycle to devise an instruction programme to teach someone to use your filing system.

Further reading

Belbin, E. and Belbin, R.M. *Problems in Adult Re-Training*, Heinemann, London, 1972.

Gagne, R.M. *Essentials of Learning for Instruction*, Holt, Reinhart and Winston, New York, 1975.

Gale, J., Das, H. and Miner, R. 'Training methods compared', *Leadership and Organisation Behaviour Journal*, Vol. 3, No. 3, pp 13-17.

Industrial Training Research Unit. *Choose an Effective Style: a Self-Instructional Approach to the Teaching of Skills*, ITRU, Cambridge, 1976.

Kolb, D.A., Rubin, I.M. and McIntyre, J.M. *Organizational Psychology: An experiential approach*, Prentice-Hall, Englewood Cliffs, New Jersey, 1974.

Tyson, S. and York, A. *Personnel Management Made Simple*, Heinemann, London, 1982.

And finally . . .

Britain's future international competitiveness and economic performance will be significantly influenced by the speed with which substantial improvements can be made in the scale and effectiveness of training by British companies. Few employers think training sufficiently central to their business for it to be a main component in their corporate strategy; the great majority did not see it as an issue of major importance – a few openly stated as much.

(Manpower Services Commission/National Economic Development Office, 1985)

43   Training – development

Training usually refers to specific activities, geared to improving the skills and knowledge needed to achieve short-term objectives, directly associated with the work to be done. An example would be training to use the new desk-top computer system. Development usually refers to less distinct objectives to do with longer term, difficult to define, aims associated with personal improvement. An example would be a development programme for leadership.

Training and development are an integral part of any work but can be resented by job holders if not felt to be appropriate. Managers may complain because they have to run their unit without the staff who are away training and individuals can be very demotivated if the training they receive is seen as a waste of time. It is also important to remember that not all problems can be solved by training. Some might be better solved by improved recruitment or investment in equipment.

A systematic approach to training and development starts with the identification of training needs. The argument is that this ensures training and development are given because they are needed. It requires an evaluation of what the present and future work involves and what the present and future staff can do. In schools a very common approach to this is a technique called GRIDS (Guidelines for Review and Internal Development in Schools), which is a series of questions about the objectives and present position of the school. Usually some training needs are identified. This process gives training needs associated with the whole organization or department. For example every member of the department will need training if quality circles are to be introduced.

Individual training needs often come from the reports on performance such as performance appraisal, assessment centres or staff report. These are discussed in Chapter 40. The reality for most organizations is that managers identify the training needs of their staff and departments far more informally.

The current approach to management training and development is to develop lists of competencies which managers need to be effective and then train or develop these. The current interest in competencies was developed by Boyatzis *(1982)* and the term includes not only skills but also mind sets and personal attributes. The lists are usually generated by committees of experienced trainers and practitioners debating what should be included.

Development techniques and methods

Lecture
A talk given without much participation by the trainees. Suitable for large audiences where the information to be got over can be worked out precisely in advance. There is little opportunity for feedback, so some may not get the point. They require careful preparation and should not be longer than forty minutes.

Talk
A talk allowing participation by the trainees, by asking questions of them or by their asking questions. Useful for getting over a new way of looking at things which require some abstraction, for example some management ideas, or views of the future. It is suitable for giving information to up to 20 people. It can work only where people are willing or able to participate. Where people do not want to participate it becomes a lecture.

Audio visual presentation
This includes slides, films and particularly video. This last technique is similar to a lecture in what it can achieve, but video has the additional advantage that you can stop and start it as often as you want.

Discussion
Knowledge, ideas and opinions on a subject are exchanged between trainees and trainer. This is particularly suitable where the application is a matter of opinion, for changing attitudes and finding out how knowledge is going to be applied. The technique requires skill on the part of the trainer as it can be difficult to keep discussion focused and useful.

Case study
This is where a history of some event is given and the trainees are invited to analyse the causes of a problem or find a solution. This provides an opportunity for a cool look at problems and for the exchange of ideas about possible solutions. However, trainees may not realize that the real world is not quite the same as the training session.

Project
Similar to an exercise but with greater freedom to display initiative and creative ideas. Projects provide feedback on a range of personal qualities. They need the full interest and cooperation of the trainee.

Group dynamics
Trainees are put into situations where the behaviour of the individuals and the group is examined. The task given to the group usually requires members to cooperate before they can achieve the objective. Observers collect information about how the trainees go about this and the feedback to the group and individuals after the task is completed. Trainees learn about the effect they have on others. This may be threatening and anxieties need to be resolved before the end of the session. Again this is very dependent on the quality of the trainer and can be dangerous if dealt with too casually.

Management competencies

Here is a short list generated by the Training Agency in 1989; each of these sections is broken down into its component parts.

---

1. Competences pertaining to dealing with *people*
   - 1.1. Those for whom one has responsibility
     - 1.1.1. Selecting
     - 1.1.2. Enabling
     - 1.1.3. Guiding
     - 1.1.4. Directing
   - 1.2. Peers, clients and customers
   - 1.3. Those to whom one reports

2. Competences concerned with *managing activities*
   - 2.4. Financial activities
   - 2.5. Systems control
   - 2.6. Techniques
   - 2.7. Functional activities

3. Competences reflecting a sensitivity to *environment and external factors*
   - 3.8. Customer expectations and needs
   - 3.9. Legal considerations
   - 3.10. Organizational, social, economic and political environment, including technological change

4. Competences reflecting *personal effectiveness*
   - 4.11. Communication
   - 4.12. Numeracy and numerical technique
   - 4.13. People orientation
   - 4.14. Results orientation
   - 4.15. Self-awareness and development

Evaluation and validation of training

If work organizations are to spend resources on training it is important to evaluate whether the training really proves useful. Hamblin *(1974)* suggests five levels on which evaluation could take place.

Reaction
The training is subjectively evaluated by the trainees on completion. They give their personal views and impressions of the value of the training.

Learning
Measure the amount of learning that has taken place in the training reliably and validly. This is what we have called validation.

Job behaviour
Assessing how much of the training has affected the work performance about six to nine months later.

Organization
The impact of training on the whole organization is measured using criteria such as productivity, time taken to do work, waste material, absenteeism, labour turnover, running costs.

Ultimate level
Trying to assess the effect of training on profitability and growth. For example some of the training in customer care in the service industry in the 1980s may account for increased profitability in this sector.

Your Management Action

Exercises

1. What method would you use to develop the competencies listed by the Training Agency? What are the advantages of doing it this way? What are the disadvantages?

2. How would you evaluate the development?

Further reading

Boyatzis, R.E. *The Competent Manager: A Model for Effective Performance*, John Wiley, Chichester, 1982.

Hamblin, A. *Evaluation and Control and Training*, McGraw-Hill, London, 1974.

Kanter, R.M. *When Giants Learn to Dance*, Unwin, London, 1989.

McMahon, A. Bolem, R. and Holly, P. *Guidelines for Review and Internal Development in Schools*, Longmans/School Council, York, 1984.

Pedler, M., Burgoyne, J. and Boydell, T. *A Manager's Guide to Self-Development*, 2nd edn, McGraw-Hill, Maidenhead, 1986.

And finally . . .

If security no longer comes from being employed, *then it must come from being* employable.

In a post-entrepreneurial era in which corporations need the flexibility to change and restructuring is a fact of life, the promise of very long-term employment security would be the wrong one to expect employers to make. But employability security *– the knowledge that today's work will enhance the person's value in terms of future opportunities – that is a promise that can be made and kept. Employability security comes from the chance to accumulate human capital – skills and reputation – that can be invested in new opportunities as they arise.*

(Kanter, *1989*, p. 321)

44 Valuing

Informally in organizations one can often hear comments such as, 'My boss doesn't value what I do', 'No one cares here', 'We are just cogs in the machine', 'I don't have the time to talk to anyone anymore'. This is even more surprising given the recent efforts in some organizations to create a culture of cooperation. Many staff generally feel unappreciated and misunderstood by their managers and others both within and without the organization.

To get the most out of our work we all need to feel that some inner need, or motivation is being met. For most of us in employment the basic needs described by Maslow, such as shelter and hunger, are met. We are looking for the higher order needs described by Maslow (see Chapter 35) of social belonging, esteem and self-actualization to be satisfied at work as there are few other arenas for most of us for these to be met.

Being appreciated or valued satisfies a combination of social and esteem needs. Appreciation is shown in a variety of ways reflecting the differences between organizations' cultures and their behavioural norms. To complicate matters, individuals feel valued in different ways. In some parts of an organization individuals may be valued by their colleagues for defying management initiatives while in other parts of the same undertaking they may be valued for closely identifying with management.

For most organizations innovation has become the norm. For individuals there is usually very little sense of 'ownership' of these changes. Individuals have to change their working practices and often take on additional work loads. It seems to us that appreciation and valuing of these efforts at an individual level is necessary if morale and contributions are to be sustained.

Making others feel valued is a complex social interaction requiring the others' views to be considered at all times. It is their needs as people, not just job holders, that have to be met. The arguments for individually determined performance related pay have tried to meet some of these needs for recognition, but for most people it is the immediate, personal contact that is as important as enhanced pay 18 months after the performance.

Consideration

We feel valued if people are considerate to us. This includes the basic etiquette of
- smiling
- asking how others are
- saying 'thank you', 'well done', 'that's great'.

It is taking an interest in what the other person is doing
- getting involved enough to discuss details
- offering resources or assistance

It is the housekeeping such as
- state of the restroom or staffroom
- coffee facilities
- cleanliness of the lavatories
- social activities.

Consultation and participation

We feel valued if we are consulted for our opinions and allowed to participate in decision making. The nature of consultation and participation is affected by

Structures such as
- the nature of the organization chart
- individuals' roles
- job descriptions

Membership of coordinating devices such as
- committees
- teams
- working parties

Processes such as
- the culture of the organization
- communication about events

Individual style of managers such as
- credibility
- accessibility
- approachability

Feedback

We feel valued if someone takes the trouble to help us find an answer to the question 'How am I doing?'

Formal ways include
- performance measurement
- performance appraisal
- review meetings

 Informal ways include
- comments
- getting repeat business.

Delegation

We feel valued when responsibility is delegated to us, not when jobs are given to us. A test of this is whether we have the responsibility to get things wrong. Delegation takes practice; the first awkward attempt should not be the reason for abandoning it. Factors to consider are:

- What are the parameters, constraints, terms of reference?
- What aspects are already decided?
- What would be quite unacceptable?
- Will they have the right to decide whether, what and how to do things?
- Who should this be delegated to?
- Am I prepared to spend more time initially to assist and develop their capacity to do the job than if I did it myself?
- How shall we keep each other informed about developments?

A case history

Alan was appearing as the main witness for his company in a court case brought by his company. They were taking one of their suppliers to court over the quality of the material. As the events in question took place several years ago it involved Alan in a lot of preparation beforehand. The court case was in London and involved him being away from home over two weeks. He was in the witness box for five days being cross-examined. During this period he was advised not to talk to anyone else about the case.

His contribution helped the company to win their case.

What would be a suitable way of showing how you valued his contribution? A letter of thanks, feedback on his contribution, a large bonus in the performance-related pay, a week's holiday?

Your Management Action

Exercises

1. In the next week see if you can find opportunities at work to say
    Thank you
    Well done
    That's great
    at least five times.

2. Look in the rest room; are there dirty cups, untidy papers, squalor? Could this be tidied up in half an hour? Why not do it?

3. In meetings do you ask for everyone's opinion? How do you hear from the quiet ones?

4. List four or five new things that have happened at work in the last few weeks. Against each indicate whether there was sufficient consultation and whether the consultation was effective.
    *   Could any of the new things have been implemented better with more or less consultation? How?
    *   List two or three innovations coming up shortly.
    *   What type of consultation would be appropriate for these?

Further reading

Fox, A. *Man Mismanagement*, 2nd edn, Hutchinson, London, 1985.
Martin, P. and Nicholls, J. *Creating a Committed Workforce*, Institute of Personnel Management, London, 1987.
Robertson, J. *Future Work*, Gower, Aldershot, 1985.
Scase, R. and Goffee, R. *Reluctant Managers*, Unwin Hyman, London, 1989.

And finally . . .

The valuing of colleagues is something for all *those in the organization to offer to each other; it is not just something for the mighty to confer on the lowly. The junior who says 'I wish I could do that' will make someone's day.*

Part E

Managing the employment relationship

45 Negotiating

In dealing with other people you cannot always get what you want. You may get less, but you could also get more than you had expected, or even more than you had thought possible. Managers spend much of their time negotiating with customers, suppliers, employees, and each other, doing deals. Some people dislike this activity, as it smacks of uncertainty, unsatisfactory compromise, fudge and bribery. 'Wheeling and dealing' suggests that you will turn in almost any direction to reach a bargain, and for some people the process of dealing can become more important than the objective at the start of the process.

There are many situations, however, that require negotiation and one of the best outcomes is where the parties both emerge from the encounter with more than they had thought of: the process of negotiating can reveal possibilities of mutual advantage that neither party individually could contemplate. In this way, your adversary becomes your helper.

Negotiations take place only when the parties need each other. One of the informal aspects of negotiation is the convention of 'shaking hands on it', implying that both parties are satisfied with the outcome: you don't shake hands with your executioner. In some situations, however, the mutual dependence is greater than others. The buyer of a Christmas present has considerable power in relation to a number of potential suppliers in being able to walk away from most of them without any personal disadvantage. The shop steward negotiating with the personnel manager cannot easily find another *management* with which to negotiate, ever though he may find another *manager* to negotiate with. When negotiators do not have a choice of adversary, negotiations are much more delicate, difficult and potentially fruitful.

Negotiation is likely to have a major, core issue. Influencing is a term used to cover a range of behaviours that are either more general or relatively minor. You influence someone to share your point of view, so that they too believe in the destruction of nuclear weapons, or that yours is the best golf club to join, or that it is high time the financial director got his comeuppance. You influence people also by persuading them to pour you a second cup of tea, lend you money, or give you a job.

Negotiation and influencing share a number of aspects of approach and skill, although negotiation is usually more formal and representative, while influencing is more informal and personal.

In employment we have collective bargaining as a means of regulating the employment relationship between employer and organized employees. To some this is the cornerstone of industrial democracy and the effective running of a business, but others see it as a poor substitute for executive action, impairing efficiency, inhibiting change and producing the lowest, rather than the highest, common factor of cooperation between management and employees. It will certainly be a poor substitute unless negotiation is conducted with a sense of purpose and confidence in what it can achieve.

Fundamental questions about preparing for negotiation

1. **Will it be negotiation or something else?**
   Negotiation is appropriate only when there is a conflict of interest between parties, who need each other to find a mutually acceptable outcome from a particular problem. The main alternatives are forcing, when you impose terms on the other party to be accepted or rejected, and problem-solving when there is a common interest and mutual support.

2. **Will it be compromise or conjunction?**
   Compromise is splitting the difference between the two parties. The seller wants £500, the buyer offers £400, and they agree on £450. This is seldom appropriate in more complex situations, as it is likely to satisfy neither party. Conjunction is exploring fully the conflicting interests of the parties and gradually putting together an agreement that provides the maximum benefits (and minimum costs) to both parties.

3. **Will the conflict be resolved or accommodated?**
   When conflict is resolved, the adversaries become friends and exchange conflict of interests for common interest. Accommodation of conflict is when the interests of the parties remain different but they find a way of working together which is to their mutual satisfaction.

4. **Is the time right?**
   For negotiation to be effective, both parties need a similar degree of interest in success. Partly this is a question of tension: are both parties under similar pressure to find a settlement? Partly it is a question of power: are the parties of roughly equal power in relation to each other regarding the negotiations that are to take place? The greater the imbalance of power between the parties, the more negative the attitudes of both: parity is most likely to bring success.

The run-up to negotiations

1. Negotiators must know and agree their objectives.
2. There must be an agenda for the meeting that both parties understand and accept.
3. Each party should have one person to present their case and question the opposing case. Other members of the negotiating team may deal with specialist matters but should not obscure the main thrust the spokesman is developing. Team members who remain silent can be very helpful in discussions among team members during adjournments.
4. The setting for the meeting should make sure that the parties face each other, reflecting their divergent interests.

The ritual of negotiation

Negotiating ritual infuriates some newcomers to the process, who see it as time-wasting, but it is an inescapable feature, with three essential phases.

In *challenge and defiance* advocates set out the position of their parties and reject the position of the other. This differentiation is a necessary preliminary to the integration and problem-solving that follows, and any antagonism is expressed as being between the parties, not between the individual negotiators. This is partly to emphasize the strength of their case, which lies in the power of those they represent ('We have a mandate from our members').

Thrust and parry marks a change. After the opening show of strength the differences are known and some idea of the relative strength of the parties is beginning to form in the minds of negotiators. There is then an almost instinctive move to the next, integrative stage, as negotiators seek out possibilities of movement and mutual accommodation. The assertiveness of challenge and defiance is replaced by more tentative comments and more listening as negotiators sound out possibilities, float ideas, ask questions, make suggestions and change their style towards a problem-solving mode. The tentative nature of any proposals is maintained by contrasting them with what was said earlier. Challenge and defiance is 'official' and authorized by the parties. Thrust and parry is 'unofficial' without any authority – yet. The negotiators are not simply revealing what they agreed beforehand. The negotiation is itself shaping the outcome, so the non-committal behaviour of the negotiators is quite genuine as a variety of possibilities are explored.

The final stage is *decision-making*. The *target point* of a negotiating team is the objective spelled out in challenge and defiance. The *resistance point* is where they would rather break off negotiations than settle. This is not declared, and it is rarely known by the negotiating team, as the point at which they *would* resist is seldom the same as that at which they *believe* they would resist. Throughout both challenge and defiance and thrust and parry the resistance points of both parties will move back and forth as different possibilities become apparent: finally they reach an agreement. What to offer, and when to offer it, is a crucial decision that is the hinge on which the negotiations will turn. It immediately renders the target point null and void, replacing it with the new offer. It is essential to get this first offer both 'right' and rightly timed because of the way in which it narrows dramatically the negotiating range. The offer may be revised, but eventually an offer is made that is accepted: but the essence of the negotiation has already taken place.

Your Management Action

Exercises

1. The last time you took part in negotiation, would it have been better for your party to have adopted a forcing or problem-solving mode? Could you have done so? How would the outcome have been different?

2. You again need your close friend to help you. Identify a valuable possession that you might be willing to sell for a suitable price – house, car, stereo system – and that your friend might be willing to buy from you. A realistic, though hypothetical, willingness on both sides is a necessary feature of selecting the possession to be 'sold'. Plan your approach for negotiating the sale, including objectives, target points and resistance points. Ask your friend to carry out similar preparation as a prospective buyer.

Conduct the negotiations, attempting to avoid simple haggling about the price. When you reach potential agreement or failure to agree, discuss your feelings about the experience.

Further reading

Atkinson, G.G.M. *The Effective Negotiator*, Quest Research Publications, London, 1977.

Fowler, A. *Effective Negotiation*, Institute of Personnel Management, London, 1986.

Kniveton, B. and Towers, B. *Training for Negotiation*, Business Books, London, 1978.

Morley, I. and Stephenson, G.M. *The Social Psychology of Bargaining*, Allen and Unwin, London, 1977.

And finally . . .

Morley and Stephenson (1977, p. 134) provide an admirable example of an inappropriate setting for negotiation, by quoting from Harold Macmillan's first impressions of an international meeting in Paris:

> The room in which we met filled me with horror the moment we entered it. The protagonists were sitting at tables drawn up in a rectangle; the space between them was about the size of a small boxing ring. But this arena was itself surrounded by rows of benches and seats which were provided, presumably, for the advisors, but seemed to be occupied by a crowd of interested onlookers. The walls were decorated with vast, somewhat confused, frescoes, depicting the end of the world, or the Battle of the Titans, or the rape of the Sabines, or a mixture of all three. I could conceive of no arrangement less likely to lead to intimate or useful negotiations. It was only when the Heads of Government or Foreign Ministers met in a small room outside in a restricted meeting that any serious discussion could take place.

46 Managing core and periphery workforces

In the 1980s organizations increasingly tended to have two categories of employee: a small core staff who have the key skills and knowledge that are crucial to the business, and a wide range of peripheral people, who may or may not be direct employees. Members of the first group are highly regarded by their employers, well paid and involved in those activities that are unique to the firm or give it a distinct character. They have good prospects and offer the employer an important contribution that cannot come from elsewhere.

Those in the peripheral category are in two broad groups: first, those who have skills that are needed but which are not specific to the particular firm, like word processing, catering or driving heavy goods vehicles; second, those with highly developed skills who are likely to be engaged on short-term contracts. This core-peripheral tendency has led to the development of many agencies, consultancies and small businesses which specialize in the supply of peripheral personnel.

The reasons for this development have been the need to be flexible – having human resources to deploy when required, while not having the responsibility and expense of continuing to employ people who are no longer needed. It has been a particularly useful strategy for dealing with contraction and innovation. Some of the advantages of 'employing' people who are in fact self-employed contractors working on your premises are: no National Insurance, sick pay, tax deduction. But the disadvantages are little commitment and difficulties deciding which jobs fall in the peripheral category.

Probably the best known examples are in the public sector of employment, with the privatization of certain services like refuse collection in local authorities and cleaning in hospitals, but the general trend has been continuing for more than 20 years. In the 1960s it was usual for companies to employ their own catering and security staff. Now the majority of in-company catering is run by contractors and nearly all security personnel are supplied by specialist firms. The employer sheds responsibility for managing the activity in which there is no in-house expertise and can obtain the benefit of rapid deployment of special expertise when needed.

Managing the peripheral staff

1. **What are they going to do?**
   - It is necessary to specify as carefully as possible what is needed.
   - This should emphasize outputs rather than inputs, what is required from them rather than how they should do it.
   - You take the 'how' for granted as they are skilled operators.
   - You will reduce their confidence and contribution if you specify the 'how' rather than the 'what'.
   - If you do not specify what is needed you lose control of your organization.

2. **Maximizing their contribution**
   - Whole jobs are better than bits and pieces as the peripheral employee can more easily see how things go together and coordinate his or her contribution.
   - Less time needs to be spent briefing them about what needs doing if there is an inbuilt logic to the various parts of their work.

3. **Commitment**
   - Peripheral staff are nearly always emotionally detached from the organization and do not have the same single minded commitment that is likely from core staff.
   - They will expect to fit their contribution to your requirements, whatever their views about culture, style, organization and so forth.
   - Attempts to involve them further may be unsuccessful as their commitment is to the job they do rather than to the organization.
   - Their personal needs are different from those of core staff and the nature of their potential contribution is also different.

4. **Everyday housekeeping**
   Guidance is needed on the everyday trivialities that everyone else takes for granted: the location of lavatories, where to go for coffee, who does the washing up, local conventions on dress, rules on discipline, car parking and so forth.

5. **The role of core staff**
   Much of the day to day managing of peripheral staff is done by core staff working alongside them. These core staff need to be valued for their contribution in enabling the peripheral staff to do a proper job.

6. **Control of their work**
   No matter how rare and mysterious the skills bought in from the periphery, those in the core must have sufficient expertise to specify and manage the peripheral contribution – otherwise there is serious risk of the tail wagging the dog.

7. **Public relations**
   Those coming into the organization, without being committed to it, also go out, taking with them an opinion about the organization.

Examples of periphery employees

George had a small barber's shop in which he employed two or three barbers apart from himself. He wanted to retire but did not have a pension plan, so he altered the way he ran the shop. He remains as proprietor and comes in to cut hair two days a week. The other three chairs are 'rented' to self-employed barbers, who pay George a weekly rent and then keep all their takings and make their own arrangements about national insurance, income tax, pension and sick pay. George provides the space, the business opportunity of a regular clientele, as well as light and heating. He is spared the worries of supervision and the three other barbers are encouraged to work quickly and maintain the goodwill of the customers.

Other examples are:
- Management consultants
- Supply teachers
- Bank nurses
- Building contractors
- System analysts on contract
- Secretarial 'temps'.

Your Management Action

Exercises

1. Which staff, core or periphery, are included by your department or
    section in the following:

    - department meetings
    - staff development
    - appraisal procedures
    - coffee clubs
    - staff outings
    - Christmas parties?

    Who is not included? Do you think this is appropriate? What do you
    think would be helpful to change?

2. What is your reaction to a new part-time or temporary employee?

    - Include them?
    - Assume someone else is looking after them?
    - Too busy to help?

3. Think of five reasons why someone might choose to be a peripheral
    employee rather than a core employee. Now think of five reasons for
    being a core employee.

Further reading

Atkinson, J. 'Management Strategies for Flexible Organisation', *Personnel
    Management*, August, 1984.
Young, H. *One of Us*, Macmillan, London, 1989.

And finally . . .

> *'One of us' is a phrase that epitomizes the Thatcher era. Originally it
> referred to an exclusive clan: 'Is he one of us?' the prime minister would
> fiercely enquire about anyone who was put up for the jobs she had to fill.
> Only those who passed the test were admitted to the band of partisans with
> whom she hoped to revolutionize Britain.*
>
> *(Hugo Young, 1989)*

47   Discrimination *

All of us discriminate between people. We have a number of stereotypes that we use simply to get through the day. If you are driving through an unfamiliar city and want to ask someone for directions, you do not stop the first person you see, you choose someone who looks likely to be helpful. Parents instruct their children not to take sweets from strangers. This may be very unfair, but nobody would suggest it should be stopped. Managers discriminate in ways which can have much more serious implications: they decide who will, and who will not, be offered a particular job, selected for further training, promotion or redundancy. Nobody would suggest that this type of discrimination should be stopped, but most would agree that it should only be done fairly. Certain forms of discrimination are acceptable, but others have been made unlawful. Discrimination in employment is inextricably linked with discrimination in the rest of society, so the law expects employers not simply to comply with strict legal requirements, but also to exercise social responsibility.

There are always groups within the employed population that are discriminated against due to the prejudices and preconceptions of the people with whom they have to deal, especially where the preconceptions are held by people who are unaware of the way they see and judge things and people. Among the less obvious preconceptions affecting employment are:

1.   Women do not want too much responsibility at work.
2.   Older people work more slowly and do not like change.
3.   People with a physical handicap are mentally disadvantaged.
4.   Qualifications gained abroad are not as good as those gained in this country.
5.   Once a thief, always a thief.

Managers have to avoid unfair discrimination partly to stay within the law and partly because they demean themselves in the eyes of their colleagues if they operate unfair and discriminatory practices. There are practical arguments as well, such as making the most of the human resources available and not wasting potential. An organization develops through the will of those who make it up. If there are people who feel they do not have fair opportunities in the organization, they will have little commitment to making things successful.

Managerial action on discrimination requires commitment to equalizing opportunity. That commitment requires not just agreement with the idea but positive, and sometimes difficult, action to make it happen.

Discrimination on grounds of sex

Features relating to preventing discrimination on grounds of sex are contained in the Equal Pay Act 1970, the Sex Discrimination Acts 1975 and 1986, the Employment Protection (Consolidation) Act 1978 and the Social Security Act 1989. The main features relating to employment are to make unlawful:

- Discriminatory advertising, recruitment, selection, promotion and dismissal;
- Sexual harassment;
- Differential payment between men and women doing the same job or work of equal value;
- Discrimination on grounds of marriage;
- Victimization of an employee who makes a complaint.

Discrimination on racial grounds

The Race Relations Act 1976 follows a similar pattern to the Sex Discrimination Acts but the unlawful acts are discrimination on the grounds of:

Race, colour, nationality or ethnic origin

Religious discrimination is not included, so there is a prohibition of discrimination against, for instance, Sikhs because of ethnic origin, but not against Jehovah's Witnesses. Segregation on racial grounds, such as the all-Indian night shift, is discriminatory.

Discrimination on age grounds

There is no legislative protection against discrimination related to age, so it is not unlawful to have arbitrary age limits for jobs, but the following are suggested as being the problems caused by age discrimination:

- Inefficient and ineffective human resourcing.
- Under-utilization of key sectors of the labour market, particularly young people, older workers, women returners and mature graduates.
- Distorted collective bargaining power for 'privileged' labour in the favoured age groups.
- Manpower planning issues of everyone retiring at the same time (IPM, 1991).

Discrimination on grounds of criminal record

The 1974 Rehabilitation of Offenders Act allows those who have been convicted of minor offences to regard them as 'spent' after an appropriate rehabilitation period has elapsed (six months for an absolute discharge, five years for a fine or community service order, seven to ten years for imprisonment of less than thirty months). They are not then obliged to disclose the conviction and it would be unlawful to deny employment to someone on the grounds of a spent conviction; there are, however, no penalties for employers who do not comply.

Discrimination on grounds of disability

The Disabled Persons (Employment) Act of 1958 provides some protection for those who are disabled. They are entitled to:

- Assessment at a rehabilitation centre and a programme of rehabilitation for up to six weeks, followed by retraining at a residential college.
- A place on the register of people with disabilities and a consequent right to a quota place with an employer.
- Certain reserved occupations (car park and lift attendants) are for registered disabled people only.

An equal opportunity check-list

Here is a quick check guide suggested by the Advisory, Conciliation and Arbitration Service (ACAS), which includes more than the basic legal obligations:

Types of discrimination
- sex
- race
- religion
- marital status
- disability
- age

Potential problem areas
- recruitment advertisements
- job requirements and selection criteria
- training (induction, apprenticeships, industrial and language training)
- promotion
- pay, hours (including overtime), pension arrangements
- job evaluation system
- grievance and disciplinary procedures
- leave (maternity, paternity, religious holidays, family sickness)
- redundancy selection
- facilities

Policy statements
- annual report
- job advertisements
- company handbook
- employment contract
- notice boards

(ACAS, *1985*)

Your Management Action

Exercises

1. Check through the equal opportunities policy in your organization, but be ready to blow the dust off it first.
   (a) To what extent do you think it has changed things?
   (b) Is there any way in which it could be made more effective?
   (c) How would you rate your organization as an equal opportunity employer?
   (d) How would you rate yourself as an equal opportunity manager?

2. Think of five people whose working performance you regard as unsatisfactory. In how many of those five cases is the unsatisfactory performance due to age, sex, ethnic origin or disability?

3. The next time you are on a train or bus, look around and mentally assign a job to each person. To what extent are your guesses guided by preconceptions of the type we have mentioned here?

Further reading

Advisory, Conciliation and Arbitration Service, *Employment Policies,* Advisory booklet No 10, ACAS, London, 1985.
Institute of Personnel Management, *Age and Employment:* An IPM Statement,
   IPM, London, 1991.
Institute of Personnel Management, *The IPM Equal Opportunities Code,* IPM, London, 1990.

And finally . . .

We hold these truths to be sacred and undeniable; that all men are created equal and independent, that from that equal creation they derive rights inherent and inalienable, among which are the preservation of life and liberty, and the pursuit of happiness.

(Thomas Jefferson, 1776)

The principle which regulates the existing social relations between the two sexes – the legal subordination of one sex to the other – is wrong in itself, and now one of the chief hindrances to human improvement . . . it ought to be replaced by a principle of perfect equality, admitting no power or privilege on the one side, nor disability on the other.

(John Stuart Mill, 1869)

48 Managing pay and performance

One basis for deciding who should be paid what is to assess what is fair. The employer believes that the employee should get a fair amount in relation to the skill and effort required and the employees feel that a fair level of pay should be given for the contribution made. Another basis for deciding pay is performance. Above average performance leads to above average pay and above average increases in pay. This has been very popular for management pay arrangements in the 1980s and is increasingly working its way down the hierarchy. This rewards output rather than input.

Some organizations have taken quite deliberate steps to manage the commitment and performance of employees. Pay has had an important part to play in this. But it is only one part of managing performance. One company has the following eight principles for managing jobs and performance:

1. A single attitude to employment and work. Every employee is part of a total business team. There is a single status about benefits and the salary scales.

2. Work is organized in the most effective way. All the techniques of job analysis and organization are brought to bear here.

3. Jobs evaluated by consistent criteria.

4. Fully informed staff. Trouble is taken over a variety of communication devices such as team briefing.

5. Fully trained staff.

6. Opportunities for personal and career development.

7. Managers responsible for their staff. They are held accountable for their section.

8. Reward for merit and performance.

Increasingly organizations have been trying to find ways of using their pay systems to reward individuals and teams for performance. The assumption is that individuals will be motivated to work for this and it will be felt fair. It also ensures that managers have to manage their staff as they are accountable for the assessment that forms the basis of the performance related pay.

Performance related pay (PRP) is a widespread phenomenon, although it has considerable problems. Satisfaction with its effectiveness is by no means guaranteed. The level of commitment in terms of time and resources, as well as the potential for it to be a demotivator for those who are only average or less, suggests it should not be entered into lightly.

Benefits of PRP

- Encourages individual initiative and responsibility
- Improves commitment of staff
- Makes for easier identification of training and development needs
- Improves job satisfaction
- Provides opportunities to harmonize working conditions
- Encourages flexible working
- Improves dialogue between supervisors and their subordinates
- Focuses on individual employee
- Improves communication in the organization

Problems of PRP

- In carrying out the appraisals
- In translating appraisals into pay
- Against team working
- Possible bias
- Inflationary tendency
- High cost of administration
- Paper work and monitoring
- Demotivating for those seen as average
- Unions may not accept
- Seen as giving senior staff pay rises at the expense of less well paid

A systematic approach to PRP

1. Derive a grade for each job using a job evaluation scheme.

2. Devise a development plan for each individual including agreed measures and objectives for both training and career development.

3. Evaluate the performance of each individual. This may be a mixture of observation and appraisal. It might be on the following criteria:
   - team working
   - decision making
   - initiative
   - creativity
   - safety
   - planning

4. Rank each individual; for example, there could be the following ranks: *unacceptable / acceptable / good / very good / excellent / exceptional*. This can be either a matter of judgement or on a weighting basis.

5. Compare the rankings with others in similar jobs to ensure that some sections are not seen as all swans and others are not seen as all swine.

6. Each individual will have a rank and this will be compared with their current position in the salary scale. Most organizations use some sort of matrix which ensures that those with a higher rank get a larger per cent salary increase than those ranked lower. However, the further up any particular scale an individual is the percentage rises get smaller. For individuals ranked low there may be no increase at all, so relative to increasing costs of living they are actually worse off.

Job evaluation

The most common scheme is that of points rating. Each bench mark job has a job description written by the job holder, by the manager of the job holder or by a job analyst. A small group then considers each description in turn. Each factor has a different weighting and each job is awarded points for each factor. The total gives the relative worth of each job. The International Labour Organisation has produced the following list of the factors most frequently used.

Accountability	Analysis and judgement
Accuracy	Complexity
Contact and diplomacy	Creativity
Decision making	Dexterity
Education	Effect of errors
Effort	Initiative
Judgement	Know-how
Knowledge and skills	Mental effort
Mental fatigue	Physical demands
Physical skills	Planning and co-ordination
Problem solving	Resources control
Social skills	Supervision given/received
Task completion	Training and experience
Work conditions	Work pressure

Responsibility for cash / materials / confidential information / equipment / process / records and reports

(ILO, *1986*)

Your Management Action

Exercises

1. What do you think your pay is rewarding you for? Attendance, being on time, length of service, doing the job described in your job description, the extras, new initiatives, or being nice to the boss?

2. Do you have PRP at your place of work? What do you feel when you get the average pay rise? Does it motivate you to do better?

3. What have been the benefits of having PRP compared to old style incremental pay rises?

Further reading

Income Data Services. *Performance Pay*, IDS Focus 49, London, 1988.
International Labour Organisation. *Job Evaluation*, ILO, Geneva, 1986.
Kinnie, N. and Lowe, D. 'Performance Related Pay on the Shopfloor', *Personnel Management*, November, 1990.
Steers, R.M. and Porter, L.W. (eds). *Motivation and Work Behaviour*, 4th edn, McGraw-Hill, London, 1989.

And finally . . .

The Regional Personnel Manager of a large clearing bank had this to say about their scheme of PRP for managers:

> It is useful for focusing the mind on objectives, but the managers themselves always ask whether they are going to get any more. I'm not sure that we are achieving a lot in the sense of people being more oriented towards specific business objectives, but the beauty of it is that we are able to keep people working till they retire instead of finding that they free-wheel for the last few years. Their pension is linked to their average earnings through the final three years of working with us, so they are very keen to keep that average up.

49 An employee relations audit

The idea of an employee relations audit is to conduct a regular check to determine how adequately employee relations practices are being performed. It is not easy to find methods of carrying out such audits that are found to be effective in practice. The most common is some form of *attitude survey*, carried out among a group of people within the organization.

The important reservation about this approach is that it raises expectation that something will happen, leading to a cynical response if the outcome is nil, or not what was anticipated.

A second approach is to have an *administrative check*, using a list of questions to establish whether you have the appropriate procedures, policies and programmes in existence that you feel are needed. This is useful to check on the inputs, but not so good as a check on effectiveness. Cuming (*1986*, pp. 411-418) is a good example of this method.

Monitoring is a method of using key indicators, like turnover and absence, as a way of auditing effectiveness of practice. The best known example of this is as advocated by the Commission for Racial Equality to check on the effectiveness of equal opportunity policies in ensuring that those from ethnic minority backgrounds obtain a fair share of promotion, training and other opportunities within the organization.

A further possibility is *modelling or mapping*, which is similar to the fault-finding approach of engineering. Here the attempt is to display diagramatically all the various elements of a process and how they interconnect. This makes it possible to review the various stages of an operation and decide where to look for weakness. This is well demonstrated by Armstrong (*1988*, pp. 32, 33, 477).

A basic, yet useful, model is SWOT analysis, whereby you list for any activity or initiative the strengths, weaknesses, opportunities and threats which exist. Having identified these features you can make plans to build on the strengths and fend off the threats.

Audit by attitude survey: an approach

1. Identify the feature of employee relations that you want to audit, define the feature as precisely as possible.

2. Decide why you want to carry out the audit and what you want to achieve. Can you handle the probable results, or should you defer until a more suitable time?

3. Identify and define the group of people who are to receive the questionnaire.

4. Draft questionnaire, considering both the objectives for the audit and the target group of respondents.

5. Test questionnaire for question sequence, clarity of questions, and value of replies. Modify and finalize.

6. Distribute questionnaires with accompanying letter of explanation or authorization, if appropriate, including how and when questionnaires should be returned.

7. Collate questionnaires, summarizing the information contained in them.

8. Analyse the information to provide:

    (a) A clear and objective summary of what is being said.
    (b) Your personal, expert interpretation of what is being said.
    (c) Plans or proposals justified by both your summary and your interpretation.

Auditing the personnel function: a check-list approach

Maurice Cuming *(1986)* suggests the following topic areas for developing a series of questions about what is being done:

Manpower plan	Personnel policies
Recruitment procedure	Induction
Contracts of employment	Training
Promotion	Transfer of employees
Dismissal procedure	Rates of pay
Job evaluation/merit rating	Working conditions
Trade union membership	Shop stewards
Joint consultation	Union recognition
Discipline	Communications
Labour turnover	Welfare services
'Staff'/'worker' differences	Health/accidents
Job descriptions	Performance standards
Assessment	Job satisfaction
Participative management	Absence
Shift working	Productivity bargains

Audit by check-list: typical questions

The section of an audit check-list dealing with communication systems within the organization might include questions like these:

1. What are the main demands on the formal systems of communication in the business?
2. What regular items of information could be removed from formal communications to avoid overcrowding?
3. What additional items should be included?
4. How can the systems be improved?
5. How can the informal systems of communication be made more effective?
6. How can the use of both formal and informal systems be improved?
7. How should the balance between face-to-face communication and distance communication (paper and electronic) be altered? How can this be done?

Audit by monitoring

Absence is often subject to audit by monitoring indicators. Here is the outline of a monitoring approach, using actual figures from the previous three months and target figures for the next three, against which actual can be plotted.

	March	April (actual)	May	June (target and actual)		July		August	
	A	A	A	T	A	T	A	T	A
1. No. of days lost									
• Management	4	4	3	2		2		2	
• Supervision & Technical	10	14	12	8		8		8	
• Admin. & Clerical	40	48	60	25		30		30	
• Shop floor	120	150	105	70		60		90	
2. Sick pay (£000)	10	12	11	9		8		5	
3. No. of temp. staff days	30	31	37	15		18		40	
4. Cost of overtime due to absence (£000)	14	16	15	5		8		14	
5. Productive efficiency (%)	88	84	92	95		95		85	
6. No. of calls at Occupational Health Service	204	180	183	150		120		100	

Your Management Action

Exercises

1. Use your personal organizer to set up an audit of your own effectiveness over the next three months.

2. Identify a specific feature of the working of your section, or yourself, which you would like to improve and use the attitude survey approach to formulate your improvement plan.

3. Produce a model or map of a specific feature of the working of your organization that you think could be improved in order to identify where the improvement could be made. If you are short of ideas, try the processes of filling vacancies or getting someone on the payroll.

Further reading

Armstrong, M. *A Handbook of Personnel Management Practice*, 3rd edn, Kogan Page, 1988.

Cuming, M.W. *The Theory and Practice of Personnel Management*, 5th edn, Heinemann, London, 1986.

Jennings, C., McCarthy, W.E.J. and Undy, R. *Employee Relations Audits*, Routledge, London, 1990.

Nobes, C. *Pocket Accountant*, Blackwell, Oxford, 1985.

Peterson, R.B. and Tracy, L. *Systematic Management of Human Resources*, Addison-Wesley, Reading, Massachussetts, 1979.

And finally . . .

Auditing is a very ancient activity. By derivation it means 'hearing' (audit is Latin for 'he hears'). Auditing was thus the original process whereby the owner heard the account given by his steward of the use of the owner's resources for the period. By the nineteenth century, the many owners of a large company would appoint one of their number to be a specific auditor of the financial statements prepared by the directors whom they had appointed to manage the company. This was partly because the process of auditing had become more complicated as business itself became more complicated.

(Nobes, *1985*)

50 Discipline and grievance

The words 'discipline' and 'grievance' have a rather jaded, Victorian sort of ring to them, lacking the drama of strategy, mission or development. Despite this they are at the heart of the employment contract. The employee who is not meeting employer expectations is liable to discipline, being reminded of what needs to be done, being ticked off for not doing it properly, warned of what will happen if the behaviour is repeated and – perhaps – penalized in some way.

The individual employee who is not satisfied with some aspect of the working situation may complain, even if this involves 'going over the head' of the immediate boss – who may well be the cause of the complaint – and trying to get a satisfactory settlement of the grievance.

Managers and supervisors fudge discipline because it involves putting their personal authority to the test and is likely to make them unpopular. People are *not* reprimanded and are *not* warned of what will happen. The manager shies away from the confrontation and the miscreant suddenly receives a memorandum terminating the contract. Instead of managing a disciplinary problem, too many managers simply get rid of it. It is weak, it is unfair, it is wasteful and the person unexpectedly facing dismissal will rightly say, 'Why didn't anyone tell me?'

In the same way aggrieved employees seldom take steps to remedy their dissatisfaction; they allow it to develop while they look for another job. When they have found the other job, they use the accumulated, brooded-upon dissatisfaction as their reason for leaving. Alternatively, they do not leave but do not express their dissatisfaction for fear of managerial revenge, afraid of becoming stereotyped as a trouble-maker. The sense of personal inadequacy about not having the nerve to complain feeds on whatever caused the original grumble, so that the person becomes less effective and thoroughly fed up.

Managers make one of their most significant contributions when they tackle problems of discipline clearly, sensitively and in good time; accepting that they are *their* problems which simply need sorting out. They are not due to fatal character defects in their subordinates.

Managers also make a significant contribution when they enable members of their section to complain, without fear of retribution. If they can also manage to satisfy a reasonable proportion of the complaints, they are well on the way to being supermanagers!

Rules

Every place of work needs to have rules, so that people know where they stand and what their employer and their colleagues expect of them. There are six types:

1. *Negligence*   is failure to do the job properly when you can. The person who is simply incompetent is not breaking the rules.
2. *Insubordination*   is either refusing to obey instructions from someone in authority or being deliberately disrespectful to such a person.
3. *Unreliability*   relates to such things as lateness or absenteeism.
4. *Theft*   is obvious when it is from another employee, but theft from the organization should be supported by very explicit rules, as some people regard taking company property for one's own use as one of the perks of the job.
5. *Interfering with the rights of others*   covers a range of socially unacceptable behaviours, such as fighting, intimidation, sexual harassment or racial taunts.
6. *Safety offences*   are those actions that can cause a hazard.

Penalties

Discipline rarely involves penalties, but they have to be available as a form of remedy when other methods are inadequate. Here are the most common:

1. *The rebuke*   is the simple reminder: 'Don't do that', or 'You can't smoke in here.' This is often all that is needed.
2. *Warnings*   present a form of remedy requiring some care as legislation has made a hierarchy of warnings an integral part of disciplinary practice. A set procedure has to be followed if the employer is to succeed in defending a claim at a tribunal of unfair dismissal. There should normally be a formal oral warning, or a written warning, specifying the offence and what is likely if it is repeated. Repetition would then lead to a final written warning that further repetition would justify a penalty such as suspension or dismissal. All written warnings should be dated, signed and kept on record for an agreed period. Details must be given to the employee and to his or her representative, if desired. The means of appeal should also be pointed out.
3. *Disciplinary transfer*   is moving the employee to less attractive work.
4. *Demotion*   is moving the employee to a different, lower status and lower paid job.
5. *Suspension*   is temporarily sending the employee home from work. This is usually for a few days with pay, either as a punishment or while an alleged offence is being investigated. An employee can be suspended without pay only if the contract of employment explicitly permits it.

A sequence for the disciplinary interview

1. Explain the management position.
2. Question to understand the employee's position.
3. Discuss to focus on the problem.*
4. Try to change the unsatisfactory behaviour by either:
    - (a) Persuasion ('You have to have an excellent attendance record if you want to move on to a job in purchasing.')*
    - (b) Disapproval ('A lot of people have said that they think you are not pulling your weight.')*
    - (c) Invoking penalties ('If this happens again, you'll be suspended.')*

The problem may be resolved at any of the points marked with an*.

5. Summarize and agree on follow-up action.
6. Move towards a close as soon as the resolution stage has been reached.

It is essential to put the matter right; simply proving that you are right and the other person wrong is of no value.

A sequence for the grievance interview

1. State what you understand the grievance to be.
2. Ask employee first to confirm that you have correctly understood the grievance, then to make the case for it.
3. Question for clarification.
4. Explain the management position.
5. Focus on the problem.
6. Discuss possibilities.
7. Decide what to do.

Three types of complaint

1. *Objective* facts about things ('The machine won't work'), with a relatively easy solution.
2. *Subjective* feelings about things ('This work is boring'), with a solution that will vary from one individual to another.
3. *Hopes and fears* coping with personal problems and challenges ('Seniority doesn't mean anything any longer'), with a solution that may be very difficult to find, and carrying major significance for the complainant.

Your Management Action

Exercises

1. Recall some complaints you have heard from people at work and classify them as objective, subjective or hopes and fears. How could those complaints have been dealt with?

2. Tina Tietjen *(1987)* identifies several difficult interviewees, including:
    (a) The artful dodger, well known at discipline interviews for fast mental footwork which he uses to distance himself rapidly from your 'case'. He knows all the tricks of the trade, and uses expressions such as, 'Well I wasn't there on that day' or 'That was the morning I had the dental appointment' or 'Didn't you get my message?'
    (b) The depressive, with the hangdog look or the 'I know I'm useless' or 'Everything's on top of me' expression that is the clue to this character. What you have to do is to decide whether it is a depression of convenience, or whether he is actually depressed.

    How would you cope with these two characters?

Further reading

Edwards, P. K. 'The Three Faces of Discipline' in Sisson, K. (ed.) *Personnel Management in Britain*, Basil Blackwell, Oxford, 1989.

Megranahan, M. *Counselling: A Practical Guide for Employers*, Institute of Personnel Management, London, 1989.

Tietjen, T. *I'd Like a Word With You*, Video Arts, London, 1987.

And finally . . .

Not quite the right approach:

At 'a well-known manufacturing company' there were protracted negotiations about a pay settlement, which ended in deadlock and there was a shop-floor decision to take strike action with effect from the following Monday. One battle-fatigued production supervisor made an announcement over the public address system in his workshop. He said that he thought the strike was quite unnecessary, but he hoped it would be orderly. The last time there had been a stoppage, a small number of trouble-makers had broken some of the lights in the perimeter fence with airguns. He was sure that there would be no such nonsense this time.

Within twenty-four hours of the strike starting, all the lamps in the perimeter fence had been broken.

51 Absence

People are away from work for a variety of reasons and for varying lengths of time. Managers tend to disapprove of this, and the term *absenteeism* has been coined to describe persistent absence. The amount of time people are away from work is increasing, partly because absence through sickness does not decrease and partly because there are an increasing number of days when absence is beyond criticism: we have longer holiday entitlement, more statutory days and more statutory time off, such as maternity leave.

Through the 1980s there was a gradual changing management attitude. Before then absence was viewed either as absenteeism, which ought to be penalized in some way, or as an Act of God, like sickness, which was beyond the control of anyone. Now we see a more thoughtful approach being taken with managers considering what the most appropriate ways are of dealing with the causes of absence. If a van driver falls while rock-climbing on his summer holiday and breaks a leg, the management can do nothing at all to alter the period of absence. On the other hand, if there is a sickness scheme which *encourages* absence, managerial attention is required immediately. There are still organizations which 'allow' x number of days uncertificated absence each year, so that there are times when the offices are almost empty due to people 'getting in their sick days' before the year end.

Absence is affected by social factors in a way that is hard to explain. The fact that shop-floor sickness absence is four times higher than management sickness absence can be partly explained by the more physically demanding nature of shop-floor work, but is that the complete explanation? The fact that those in Wales have three times as many days off annually as those in the South East is partly explained by regional health variations, but is that all?

Absence is caused by a variety of factors and it can be managed only by thorough analysis. Management attention to absence is therefore one of the most basic of management tasks, looking after efficiency and looking out for the people who work in the section.

How absent are the British?

It is notoriously difficult to compare social statistics across national boundaries because the means of collecting data vary, but the most reliable recent comparative data (Klein, *1983*, using figures from the European Community's 1983 Labour Force Survey) show the following national absence rates:

Belgium	3.8%	France	5.9%
Holland	5.4%	Germany (West)	3.0%
Italy	2.9%	Japan	2.5%
Sweden	3.0%	United Kingdom	11.8%

Which Brits are missing?

The General Household Survey includes a wealth of interesting information about British life. The 1984 survey found that 7 per cent of the working population had been absent in the previous week for widely differing reasons. The percentage varied for different types of job:

- 3% Managers in small establishments
- 5% Managers in large establishments, professionals
- 6% Unskilled manual workers
- 7% Non manual and personal service workers
- 8% Agricultural workers
- 9% Supervisors, semi-skilled manual workers
- 10% Skilled manual workers

What does absence cost?

ACAS estimate that 370 million working days are lost every year through certificated absence alone, and point to the following aspects of cost incurred:

excessive demands on the sick pay scheme, overmanning, excessive overtime, replacement labour, lost or delayed production, reduced range or standard of service, disruption of the flow of work, low morale and general dissatisfaction, resulting in low productivity.

The Steers and Rhodes process model of attendance

The most thorough review of research on absence behaviour is that conducted by the Americans Steers and Rhodes *(1978)*. They found two main limitations in the previous research. First it nearly always started from the assumption that absence was mainly caused by job dissatisfaction; second that employees had free choice of whether to attend work or not. Neither of these assumptions is accurate for all circumstances, so Steers and Rhodes *(1978)* produced a process model to explain the causes of absence in terms of the pressures to attend and the situational constraints. The model is shown below.

The Steers and Rhodes Model of Employee Attendance

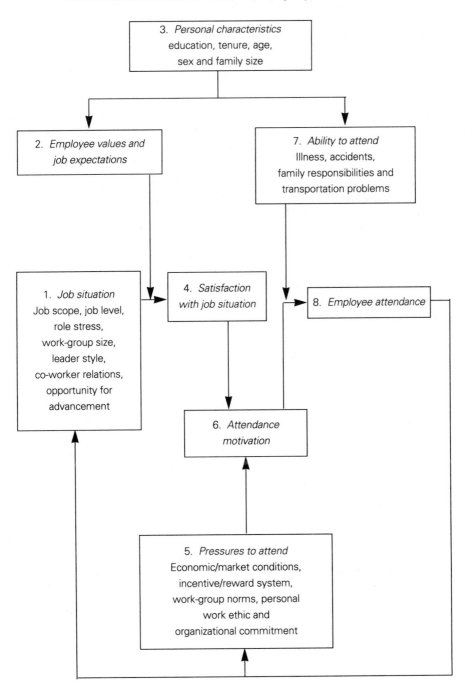

Your Management Action

Exercises

1. Identify a section of the organization where you think absence is relatively high, and then use the formulae described in Chapter 31 on Personnel Indicators to measure the absence level.
2. Use the Steers and Rhodes process model on the previous page to analyse the situation you have identified. Decide what to do.

Further reading

Advisory, Conciliation and Arbitration Service. *Absence, Advisory Booklet No. 5*, ACAS, London, 1983.

Edwards, P. K. and Whitston, C. *The Control of Absenteeism*, University of Warwick, Warwick, 1989.

Huczynski, A. A. and Fitzpatrick, M. J. *Managing Employee Absence for a Competitive Edge*, Pitman, London, 1989.

Incomes Data Services. *Absence Control*, IDS Study No. 403, IDS, London, 1988.

Klein, B. 'Missed Work and Lost Hours', *Monthly Labour Review*, May, 1983.

Sargent, A. *The Missing Workforce*, Institute of Personnel Management, London, 1989.

Steers, R.M. and Rhodes, S.R. 'Major influences on employee attendance', *Journal of Applied Psychology*, Vol. 63, No. 4, 1978, pp. 391-407.

And finally . . .

Huczynski and Fitzpatrick (1989) suggest the ALIEDIM approach to absence control:

- *Assess the absence problem*
- *Locate the absence problem*
- *Identify and prioritize the absence causes*
- *Evaluate the current absence control approaches*
- *Design the absence control programme*
- *Implement the absence control programme*
- *Monitor the effectiveness of the absence control programme*

On the other hand . . .

Absence makes the heart grow fonder.

(Anon.)

52 Dismissal

Every employer has the right to dismiss an employee: none of us has a right to employment beyond what is specified in our individual contract. Employers cannot, however, dismiss any of their employees whimsically: every employee has the right not to be *unfairly dismissed* although the extent of that protection varies with length of service and terms of contract.

Unfair dismissal has to be understood as a legal term rather than in its common sense meaning. The employer must have a fair ground for dismissal, as defined in the Employment Protection (Consolidation) Act of 1978, and the dismissal should be in accordance with an understood procedure. Also an employee must actually have been dismissed before a complaint can be lodged. The employee has no legal right, as in some other countries, to have the dismissal suspended until its legality has been decided.

Every employee acquires the right to protection against unfair dismissal after two years of continuous employment with the employer against whom the complaint may be laid, providing that the employment is for at least 16 hours a week. Those working between eight and 16 hours a week acquire the protection after five years' continuous employment. This two-year qualifying period does not apply to dismissals on the grounds of trade union membership, race or sex.

Any employees believing they have a justifiable claim for unfair dismissal have to make a claim to an Industrial Tribunal within three months of the effective date of termination. The claim will then be referred to ACAS for conciliation. The ACAS official may explain to the aggrieved employee that the dismissal was not unfair or that the claim is technically flawed in some way. Alternatively there may be a conciliated agreement between the parties, who decide to cut their losses. It is only the minority of cases that actually proceed to a tribunal hearing, as the following figures from ACAS annual reports indicate.

	1983	1990
Cases received for conciliation	37,123	37,584
Settled by ACAS	15,591	22,516
Withdrawn	9,171	6,333
To tribunal	12,575	6,376

The decision of the tribunal could be to dismiss the claim, to accept the claim and recommend reinstatement or re-engagement, or to order compensation. Reinstatement or re-engagement is rarely accepted by the parties, so the compensation remedy is by far the most common.

What is a fair ground?

A dismissal is potentially fair if there is a fair ground for it. Such grounds are:

1. *Lack of capability or qualification*
    If an employee lacks the skill, physical capacity, aptitude or necessary qualifications to do the job. As the employee acquires protection against unfair dismissal only after two years, what have the management done in that period to remedy the lack of capability?

2. *Misconduct*
    This category covers the range of actions that are well known, such as disobedience, unjustified absence, insubordination and criminal acts. It can also include taking industrial action.

3. *Redundancy*
    Where an employee's job ceases to exist, it is potentially a fair ground for dismissal.

4. *Statutory bar*
    When employees cannot continue to discharge their duties without breaking the law, they can be fairly dismissed. Almost invariably the operation of this category is for drivers who have been disqualified from driving for a period.

5. *Some other substantial reason*
    This most intangible category was introduced in order to cater for genuinely fair dismissals that were so diverse that they could not realistically be listed. Examples have been security of commercial information (where an employee's husband set up a rival company) and employee refusal to accept altered working conditions.

Having decided whether or not a fair ground existed, the tribunal then considers two further questions:

- Was the decision *reasonable* in the circumstances?
- Was the dismissal carried out in line with the *procedure*?

Dismissal for incapacity through sickness

Selwyn *(1985,* p. 241) lists nine questions that have to be answered to decide the potential fairness of dismissing someone on grounds of ill-health:

(a) how long has the employment lasted, (b) how long had it been expected the employment would continue, (c) what is the nature of the job, (d) what was the nature, effect and length of the illness, (e) what is the need of the employer for the work to be done, and to engage a replacement to do it, (f) if the employer takes no action, will he incur obligations in respect of redundancy payments or compensation for unfair dismissal, (g) are wages continuing to be paid, (h) why has the employer dismissed (or failed to do so) and (i) in all the circumstances, could a reasonable employer have been expected to wait any longer?

Constructive dismissal

If the behaviour of the management causes a person to resign, the ex-employee may still be able to claim dismissal on the grounds that the behaviour of the employer constituted a repudiation of the contract, leaving the employee with no alternative but to resign; the employee may then be able to claim that the dismissal was unfair. The employer's conduct must amount to a significant breach, going to the root of the contract, such as physical assault, demotion, unilateral reduction in pay, change in location of work or significant change in duties.

If a tribunal finds that an employee has been constructively dismissed, it may not necessarily decide that the dismissal was unfair.

Compensation for dismissal

If the tribunal upholds an employee's claim of unfair dismissal, and if re-engagement or reinstatement are not suitable remedies, they can consider four types of financial compensation.

1. *The basic award* This is calculated in the same way as redundancy pay: ½ week's pay for each year employed by the employer between the ages of 18 and 21, 1 week's pay for each year between ages 22 and 40, 1½ weeks' pay for years between 40 and 64.

2. *The compensatory award* The tribunal will add an amount to compensate the employee for financial loss resulting from the dismissal. There is a maximum for compensation, which is adjusted annually.

3. *A special award* of between 13 and 26 weeks' pay may be made where an employer refuses to abide by a recommendation for reinstatement or re-engagement. Unfair dismissal on grounds of union membership, race or sex can attract an additional award of between 26 and 156 weeks' pay.

Wrongful dismissal

Long before the 1971 Industrial Relations Act first introduced the concept of unfair dismissal, employees had enjoyed the common law right of protection against wrongful dismissal. Claims are brought in a County or High Court and relate to cases where it is alleged that the dismissal was in breach of the contract of employment between the two parties, usually where the employee is dismissed without notice or with a period of notice shorter than that specified in the contract.

Your Management Action

Exercises

1. Consider the working activities of some of your colleagues. What examples can you find of behaviour that you feel justifies dismissal on grounds of organizational efficiency? How many of these could be described as fair grounds for dismissal? If these people were dismissed, which dismissals would be generally approved of by your other colleagues and yourself, and which would you deplore?

2. In the examples you noted in the above exercise, how many of those dismissed do you think would prefer reinstatement to financial compensation? In how many cases do you think the employer would consider reinstatement?

3. Attend a tribunal hearing and decide what your judgement would be if you were the tribunal. Then listen to their judgement and see where you (or they) went wrong.

Further reading

Advisory, Conciliation and Arbitration Service. *Annual Reports*, ACAS, London, 1983, 1990.
Incomes Data Services. *Unfair Dismissal*, IDS, London, 1988.
Lewis, D. *Essentials of Employment Law*, 3rd edn, Institute of Personnel Management, London, 1990.
Selwyn, N. *Law of Employment*, 5th edn, Butterworth, London, 1985.

And finally . . .

A woman with a poor record of sickness absence was given time off for a gynaecological operation. She was also warned that any further time off in the following six months would lead to dismissal. Two months later she was dismissed after going in to hospital where she had a miscarriage. The employer contended that the dismissal was fair because pregnancy was not the principal reason for the dismissal. The tribunal found the dismissal unfair on the grounds that she would not have been dismissed if she had not had a miscarriage, which was a reason connected with pregnancy.

(George v. Beecham Group Ltd, *1976*)

53 Contracts of employment

All those who are *employees* of an employer are entitled to, and bound by, a contract of employment. Others doing the employer's work may be bound by a contract for services; only employees are subject to a contract of employment, which specifies the mutual obligations of the parties. Basically the employee provides time and effort as required by the employer who provides payment in return. The employee, however, also has specific rights to certain things, such as safe working conditions, sick pay, payment of wages rather than a lump sum, the deduction of income tax and national insurance contributions, and the range of statutory rights ranging from protection against unfair dismissal to rights in relation to trade union membership. The contract may be made orally or in writing, but a written statement of key elements in the contract must be provided to the employee within 13 weeks of the contract beginning.

Although the normal (Department of Employment) means of defining full-time workers is that they work 30 hours a week or more, all those who work 16 hours a week or more have the legal rights of full-time workers. Those who work between eight and 16 hours acquire these rights only when they have been in continuous service with the employer for five years.

Part-time workers frequently enjoy lower rates of pay than full-timers. Employers are not legally obliged to pay them the same as those working full time, but they are bound by the Equal Pay Act, so that part-timers could have a claim for equal pay if they can identify a full-time worker of the opposite sex carrying out similar work.

Theoretically the terms of the contract are individually negotiated, but in the majority of cases the terms are as specified by the employer, with the employee having the right to reject rather than vary the terms, apart from a possible modification of the pay level. Some terms can also be derived from collective agreements with recognized trade unions, although those agreements do not have legal standing. Many contracts include such phrases as 'conforming to the national agreements for the time being in force between X employers' association and Y trade union'. A further contractual element can be the use of company rules. The need for the employee to comply with the rules of the workplace is always implicit, as the contract of employment is rooted in the common law tradition of the servant obeying the master, but there may be an explicit reference to such rules, which an employer can change at will, whereas terms of a collective agreement can be varied only by agreement between the parties.

The present legal definition of a contract of employment is in section 153 of the *Employment Protection (Consolidation) Act* of 1978.

What the contract should contain

Employees have to be supplied with written particulars of their main contractual terms within 13 weeks of starting employment. The essential features are:

(a) The names of employer and employee
(b) The date on which the employee's period of continuous employment began
(c) The rate and interval of payment
(d) Hours of work and the normal times of such work
(e) Holidays and holiday pay
(f) Arrangements for sick pay and sickness absence
(g) Pension provision
(h) Periods of notice
(i) Job title
(j) Arrangements for dealing with employee grievances

Implied terms

Not everything that is contractually binding is written in the contract. All are deemed to have certain features in them that can be implied if not made explicit:

(a) The parties will cooperate with each other to maintain mutual trust and confidence;
(b) They will act in good faith towards each other;
(c) They will take reasonable steps to make sure that the workplace is safe and healthy.

Truck Acts

In the late eighteenth century there was a shortage of small denomination coins, so some employers paid their employees in kind or with tokens that could be exchanged for goods only at the factory shop. The Truck Acts were passed to outlaw this practice, requiring all employers to pay their manual workers in coin of the realm. It was not until the late 1980s that this Act was finally repealed, so now all employees can be paid by cheque or by credit transfer if the employer so chooses. There are, however, a dwindling number of employees who are deemed to have established a *contractual right* to payment in cash because of practice obtaining before the repeal of the Truck Acts. Moving them to 'cashless pay' without their consent would be breach of contract.

Annual hours contracts

The concept of normal working hours is crucial to the interpretation of the contract, especially when overtime may be worked. Some organizations have moved to greater flexibility by introducing annual hours contracts, which may reduce costs and improve performance. The period of time within which full-time employees must work their contractual hours is defined over a whole year. An average 38-hour week, for example, becomes 1732 annual hours, assuming five weeks' holiday entitlement. Within agreed criteria, employees then undertake to deliver their annual complement at mutually acceptable times.

The main advantage in manufacturing companies seeking to maximize the utilization of expensive assets, comes from separating employee working time from the operating hours of the plant and equipment. Lynch *(1988,* p. 137) provides an example:

> a company that is operating a three shift system on a 37 hour week (Monday to Friday) may currently use weekend hours at premium rates to meet extra production, this being the only flexible option available. A move to six-day working (i.e., from 112 operating hours to 144) would increase production by 28%. A move to seven-day working would increase production by 50%.

Employee attitudes to annual hours contracts vary. There are all the advantages of flexibility in being able to concentrate work time and leisure time separately. This is increasingly feasible as the normal working week drops down below 38 hours. Many people are keen to work eight or ten hour days in order to maximize time off. There is, however, a greater degree of detachment from the social system of the workplace and the loss of a predictable weekly pattern of work and leisure.

Self-employment

A further development is where the employee ceases to be an employee at all, and is self-employed. At first sight, this is often an attractive proposition for the employer, who loses the responsibility of national insurance contributions, sickness pay and the moral obligation of an employer towards employees. If business is bad there is no problem of redundancy payments and if the job is not being done well, there is no worry about unfair dismissal. Employees are not all so keen on the idea because of the greater insecurity and the increased administrative duties of the self-employed. The notion of being your own boss is, however, very attractive to some, who also feel there is greater security in providing services to a number of employers than in being wholly dependent on one.

Your Management Action

Exercises

1. Review your own contract of employment. In what ways does it fall short of what you would regard as ideal? What would you like to see made explicit that at the moment is only implicit – or missing altogether?

2. Review your contract of employment again, but looking at it from the perspective of your employer rather than yourself. How reasonable do you now think your original ideas of change are?

Further reading

Advisory, Conciliation and Arbitration Service. *Employing People*, ACAS, London, 1985.

Lewis, D. *Essentials of Employment Law*, 3rd edn, Institute of Personnel Management, London, 1990.

Lynch, P. 'Matching Worked Hours to Business Needs', *Personnel Management*, June, 1988.

Rothwell, S. 'How to Manage from a Distance', *Personnel Management*, September, 1987.

Stanworth, J. and Stanworth, C. 'Home truths about teleworking', *Personnel Management*, November, 1989.

And finally . . .

Industrial action and the employee's contractual duty not to impede the employer's business:

> In the leading case of Secretary of State v ASLEF, *which involved a work to rule on the railways, the Court of Appeal gave different reasons in reaching the conclusion that such a duty exists. Lord Justice Roskill thought that there is an implied term that employees ought not to obey lawful instructions in such a way as to disrupt an employer's business. Lord Justice Buckley extended the notion of fidelity and proclaimed that 'the employee must serve the employer faithfully with a view to promoting those commercial interests for which he is employed.' Lord Denning chose to focus on motive, i.e. the wilfulness of the disruption caused, and his formulation leads to the conclusion that all forms of industrial action are likely to be unlawful. More recently the High Court has ruled that it is a professional obligation of teachers to cooperate in running schools and that the failure to cover for absent colleagues amounts to a breach of contract.*
>
> (Lewis, 1990, p. 36)